THE BOY WITH THE KNAPSACK

THE BOY WITH THE KNAPSACK

An Extraordinary Life, from the Kindertransport to the House of Lords

LORD ALF DUBS

ITHAKA

First published in the UK in 2026 by Ithaka Press
An imprint of Bonnier Books UK
5th Floor, HYLO, 105 Bunhill Row,
London, EC1Y 8LZ

A CIP catalogue record for this book is available from the British Library.

Hardback ISBN: 978-1-80617-382-2
Also available as an ebook and an audiobook

1 3 5 7 9 10 8 6 4 2

Design and Typeset by Envy Design Ltd.
Printed and bound in Great Britain by CPI (UK) Ltd, Croydon CR0 4YY

MIX
Paper | Supporting responsible forestry
FSC® C013604

At Bonnier Books UK, we are committed to publishing sustainably. Find out more here:
bonnierbooks.co.uk/sustainability

The authorised representative in the EEA is
Bonnier Books UK (Ireland) Limited.
Registered office address:
Block B, The Crescent Building
Northwood, Santry
Dublin 9, D09 C6X8
Ireland
compliance@bonnierbooks.ie

www.bonnierbooks.co.uk

For Ann Dubs

CONTENTS

PROLOGUE

Looking back on my life, I am struck by its many contrasts. In my childhood, I lived through persecution and displacement, but on coming to the UK, I also experienced enormous generosity and acceptance. In my work in Northern Ireland, I saw political violence drive groups apart, but also witnessed the transformative power of reconciliation. And in today's debates about refugees and migrants, I've often heard the rhetoric of fear and hatred, but I've also seen the human decency and kindness that strangers can be met with in this country.

Throughout my career, I have met many men and women of power; people with famous names and faces that you would recognise on the street. It is thrilling to be close to those individuals, to be at the centre of things, to wake up each day and walk into the magnificent buildings of our Parliament and think, 'Can this really be me? How lucky I am.'

But if I am honest, looking back, it is not those faces and

names that I remember most clearly. Over the decades, I met so many people who worked tirelessly to make the world a better place; people who campaigned for the rights of the vulnerable, who dedicated endless energy to improving their communities, and who were deeply devoted to making society fairer. Most of those individuals were not famous, and they didn't want to be. But they are the ones who really deserve to be remembered.

I am in my nineties, and my memories of British life and history span nearly a century. There are many things that I have learned over the course of my career. But perhaps the most enduring one is that politics can still be a force that unites people, that reminds us of our humanity and encourages us to set our differences aside to look to the future. I hope that is a message readers can take from these pages.

Part One

REFUGEE

I.

I arrived in England, at Liverpool Street station in London, on 30 June 1939, with around 150 or 200 other children. I was six years old, and so my memories of that long journey from Prague are slight, though shot through with images that remain vivid, nearly eighty-seven years later.

I still don't know how it was that I was able to escape Czechoslovakia by train. There was much demand to get on the Kindertransport, as it was called. Perhaps it helped that my father had already reached England. Many of the other unaccompanied children with whom I travelled were granted entry to the UK on condition that a foster family was found to meet them and look after them, until such a time as they could return home or be reunited with their parents. Of course, for some, that day would not come.

I'd just started school when my mother said she would put me on a train to London, where I would be met by my father. I hadn't seen him for three months, and so my mother emphasised this to soften the blow of leaving her and assuage some of my fears. I couldn't fully understand what was happening but sensed something was going to change profoundly for us. She packed some food for the journey in a small knapsack. Once on the train, I was given a thin cardboard luggage tag to wear – all the children had one to identify them, ready for our arrival in London.

Even now, I can clearly see in my mind my mother standing on the platform at Prague station with a friend waving me off, along with many other parents, looking anxious. Also the German soldiers in uniforms, swastikas on their arms. One in particular was watching them. Some soldiers came onto the train and entered a few carriages; they tipped the luggage out and checked it, but not mine. Eventually, at around eight in the evening, the train left. I wonder how much I understood about what was going to happen next.

I can't recall the pain of saying goodbye to my mother. She was planning to leave Prague too and join my father and me in London, but she first had to get the relevant paperwork from the new Nazi government. She had been refused an exit permit at what was probably a Gestapo office. Two German soldiers had then thrown her down the stairs, where she landed in a heap at the bottom. Before working out whether anything was broken, she realised that they had thrown her passport after her, rather than kept it, which gave her some hope that she would find a way out. In the meantime, she had heard of the

Kindertransport and made what must have been a difficult decision that I should go ahead without her.

I was in the grip of fate. There is nothing in my memory that tells me how stressed I felt. I think I was bewildered and uncertain but stoical. I didn't know anyone else on the train and can't remember talking to anyone on the journey. It is not clear why we remember some things from our childhood and others fade. Perhaps these memories have been lost to time or I shut everything out because it was so traumatic. I don't know.

We travelled in carriages of six to eight children. I was one of the youngest. We had hard wooden seats on which to sit, but, as children, it was no great hardship for us. Though it seemed an interminably long journey.

There was a problem with documents at the Czech–German border that caused a lengthy delay. By the time we reached the Dutch border, around a day after leaving Prague, it was dark again. The older children on the train cheered when we crossed the frontier. I didn't know why but sensed that something important was happening. I thought I might see windmills and wooden shoes, which was all I knew about Holland. Only afterwards did I understand that they were cheering because we had reached safety from the Nazis. It was a little less than a year before the short-lived Battle of the Netherlands, which ended with the Dutch government surrendering to the Nazis and a new wave of desperate refugees looking for escape.

Eventually, we reached the Hook of Holland where we took a boat to Harwich. I had never seen the sea before. There were two bunks in the cabin. I was in a lower bunk, with an older boy in the bunk above. Somehow, I did fall asleep. When I woke up in the morning, I was in Harwich harbour, my first sight of England. Doctors came on board to examine us before we disembarked for the train to Liverpool Street station.

As we approached Liverpool Street, I was leaning out of the window and was spotted by my father. As soon at the train came to a halt, he rushed over to greet me. He tried to hug me but was stopped by a police officer who said that we mustn't mix until they had checked everyone off.

We entered a large room in the station. One by one, each child was ticked off and handed over to the family member or foster family who had come to meet us at the station. We were still wearing our luggage tags, identifying us. I felt a huge sense of relief at seeing my father. But I don't think I realised at that age how much luckier I was than many of the children on the Kindertransport, who were met by strangers. Some children never saw their parents again, others only after their parents had escaped, sometimes via the Far East. Years later, I heard the scene at Liverpool Street on the arrival of the Kindertransport trains described as 'utter chaos'. I can imagine that would be true – what with volunteers having so many bewildered children to unite with foster families. But I cannot recall it.

At last, I could step out into this strange new city with my father. He took me back to his bedsitter in Belsize Park in north London, where we would live while we awaited news of my mother; whether she had been able to get the right papers to leave Prague and join us. When he unpacked my small knapsack, he was surprised to find the food my mother had packed for the journey. An older boy had looked after me on the boat, but he had never suggested I eat anything – it's possible that I didn't, all the way to England. Although I was a boy with a good appetite. Either way, my father was delighted to be able to eat peppery Czech sausages – an involuntary ex-pat enjoying the food from home. A small consolation, perhaps, in such uncertain times.

My parents were born in Austria-Hungary before the First World War. My father's family came from northern Bohemia, although he was born in Vienna. Both his parents died young, so I never knew them. My mother, Bedřiska (also known as Frieda), came from southern Austria, near Carinthia. My father's family was Jewish but my mother's family wasn't. We were a secular family, although I had no idea about religion or what it meant to be observant – or not until much later. I believe that my parents met when my dietician mother was professionally advising my overweight father.

I was born on 5 December 1932 in Prague. My parents lived in a large flat in Holečkova in Smíchov, a mixed area. I think we lived on the second floor. Life was comfortable, though we were not wealthy. My father was employed in the cotton industry with his cousins. I saw a lot of them because they also lived in Prague and we were very close to them.

In winter, hoses were used to flood tennis courts so they would become ice rinks for skating. In summer, my parents would take me on holiday to Austria, on the Wörthersee, a lake in southern Austria. Our last holiday there was in 1937, when I was four and a half. I heard shooting on the other side of the lake, apparently caused by some Nazi supporters. We didn't go back the next year; most likely because of the rising tide of Nazism in the country. We went to Hungary instead. There, I ran along the swimming jetty and caught a large splinter in the sole of my foot. The local doctor tried to take it out but on returning to Prague, my foot was still sore. The woman who occasionally came to help us around the house took one look, found a leaf growing at the back of the property and strapped it to my foot. The next day the large splinter came out; I would love to know what the leaf was!

My father, Hubert Dubs, served in the Austro-Hungarian army during the First World War. First on the Western Front against the British, where he took part in the Christmas Day ceasefire in 1914. He told me that he had swapped cigars with a British officer in the middle of no man's land. He was then sent to Italy and fought on the Isonzo – a river valley now in Slovenia and the scene of many battles and huge loss of life between 1915 and 1917. He was injured, he was gassed, and he came back with a few medals.

Throughout my childhood, his hatred of war was such that I was never allowed to have guns or tanks to play with. All my friends had plenty of such toys, but I had to make do with a tractor. Then, one day, after we had arrived in London and war between Britain and Germany been declared, my father went out and came back with a box of tin soldiers for me. As a six-year-old I was delighted. A long time after his death, I realised the awful significance of that gift. It was a sign of despair that there was yet another war. He knew what that meant from his own experience. I don't think he was a pacifist because he also knew what Nazism meant. Indeed, he tried to join the Home Guard at one point but as a foreigner was not allowed to do so, despite his military experience.

The Nazis occupied Austria, the country of my parents' birth, on 12 March 1938. The annexation was known as the 'Anschluss' and was the first major expansion of the Nazis in their push to gain more territory. They received an enthusiastic welcome from much of the population, who saw themselves as ethnically German. The persecution of the country's Jewish population began immediately. Not long after the occupation began, my mother visited friends in Vienna. No doubt fearful for my father, and worried about what it might mean for our family if the Nazis came to Prague, she and my father wanted to find out what was happening. My mother's friends drove her to the edge of the city, kept the engine running and told her what the Nazis were doing. They kept the engine running because they were afraid that the Nazis would be eavesdropping on their conversation, even though methods of surveillance in those days were not as sophisticated as they are today. Such was the level of fear.

I later learned that my father had discussed it with his cousins and told them that if the Nazis occupied Prague, he would leave. Was his decision to flee Czechoslovakia immediately on the German occupation influenced by what my mother learned in Austria about how the Nazis were treating Jewish people? What did he know or think might happen, bearing in mind that the full horrors of Nazi rule were not so obvious at that point?

The Nazis occupied the Sudetenland in October that year. By then, it was clear what was going to happen. German troops marched into Prague early in the morning on 15 March 1939 and, true to his word, my father left the city within a day of the Nazis' arrival. He left quickly and discreetly, but I had been aware, as children often are, of the growing tension in our house. My father was not a political man and I never discovered why he took such a decisive step when many of our family and friends did not. His two cousins, with whom he worked, said they would take their chances. Tragically, in 1942, the Gestapo came for them; one was taken to Auschwitz and the other swallowed a cyanide pill.

My father travelled for work and had been to England and Scandinavia not long before the Nazi occupation, which might have influenced his choice of city. He had a little English but not much. Perhaps he still had an active visa that allowed him to travel there. Otherwise, I don't know why he chose London. Though of course this decision was to have the most profound impact on my life.

Every single refugee who has ever fled their home is a person who has had to make an impossible decision, and it is hard to fully comprehend now the choices facing people at that time. As the restrictions on Jews increased and then the deportations started, some did escape, either legally or illegally. But for those without family or friends abroad, or lacking the means to get out, it was less clear what to do for the best. For many of those from sheltered, comfortable backgrounds, going on the run seemed unimaginable. Our neighbour in the flat below was a Jewish bank manager. After I left Prague, at about 4 a.m. one morning, there was a loud banging on his door. Contrary to usual practice, the Gestapo did not smash the door down; they returned three hours later, by which time the man had fled. He stayed on the run for two weeks before – out of ideas or unable to cope – he gave himself up. My mother told me this story some years later. His son, who possibly also escaped on a Kindertransport, went to the same school I attended in Wales, some years ahead.

Hitler paid his first visit to Prague soon after it was occupied by the Germans. Schools were supposed to send their children to the city centre to 'celebrate' our new leader. However, my mother complained that we were all too young and, as a result, my class did not go. Though we all had to tear a picture of President Beneš out of the front of our textbooks and replace it with a picture of Hitler. Suddenly there were German soldiers everywhere, strutting visibly in the streets.

*

The first Kindertransports were organised in the wake of Kristallnacht, the wave of anti-Jewish violence and rioting that swept Germany and Austria in November 1938, instigated and encouraged by the Nazi party. With reports growing of Jewish people being taken off to 'camps', of which little was known, the British government agreed to allow unaccompanied children and teenagers into Britain on a 'temporary' basis, but it would not pay for their board – individual people and charitable organisations did this. The first trains left from Berlin and Vienna the following month, with Jewish organisations in those cities deciding which children were the priority.

Meanwhile, a stockbroker from London called Nicholas Winton was supposed to be on a skiing holiday in Switzerland when a friend told him that he should visit Prague as there was a serious situation emerging with Jewish refugees from the recently occupied Sudetenland. He was taken to meet some refugees and learned of the terrible plight of the children.

When the German army occupied the remainder of Czechoslovakia in March 1939, Nicky realised the need to help the country's Jewish children had become even more urgent. He organised a series of trains to take the children to Britain. But before that he had to persuade the British government to accept them, which he succeeded in doing, although few governments had been willing to help.

Of course, Nicky had a team of helpers in Prague. They organised the trains when Nicky was back in the UK, making arrangements to receive the children, finding parents or foster parents to look after them there. The British government also demanded that a guarantee of £50 was paid for each unaccompanied child – the equivalent of nearly £3,000 these days, so funds had to be raised in many cases. Nicky not only had to deal with the British government but the Nazis too. However, he was highly resourceful. On one occasion, some crucial documents were late in arriving, so Nicky simply forged the signatures to prevent that train of children from being delayed. The Nazi administration also at one point set a woman spy on him to see if they could find out more about what he was doing.

It is significant that he did not have to do it. He saw that there was a problem, an urgent humanitarian problem, and decided he would devote himself to helping children to escape. A lesser person would have simply thought, *It's nothing to do with me*, and carried on with their own life. But Nicky was made of sterner stuff and was very determined. The Kindertransports that he and his team organised from Prague brought 669 children to London, the majority of whom were Jewish and would have almost certainly otherwise not have survived the Holocaust.

I was aware that I had arrived on the Kindertransport, though I don't know by what stroke of good fortune – or perhaps it was my mother's resourcefulness and perseverance. And I would meet other children from Prague who had arrived the same way. But I knew nothing about Nicky Winton for many years. Very few people did until much later. Nicky volunteered to become an ambulance driver after the outbreak of the Second World War, and was in the RAF. He continued to help people when he could throughout his life, believing it was simply the right thing to do, and barely ever spoke of his tireless efforts in those months before the start of the war. It wasn't until the 1980s that the story came to the attention of the public, and I, along with lots of other 'Nicky's children', learned about this remarkable man who had stepped in to save our lives. By then, many of us had children and grandchildren who wouldn't have existed without his efforts.

In London, my father was going through a terrible time. War seemed inevitable and my mother was yet to escape German-occupied Prague. He was very worried about her, had limited money and was wondering what work he would have. A small consolation was that many of the Jews who had arrived in London at that time were also living nearby in Belsize Park and would come to say hello. Many were like us, having escaped the Nazis in our homelands and were now facing the same anxieties.

My father wanted me to learn English, so he put me in a small school for refugee children in Sydenham. It was quite a trek, but the only place he could find that would teach me the language. I had to board at the school during the week. It was a long way from our small bedsit, which, besides, didn't have room for both of us. I hated the long journey to school, involving a few different buses, as it meant leaving my father for days at a time – again, I was being uprooted and sent away from family to strangers and unknown environments. Once, I was sick on the bus on the way there. At least I could spend the weekends with my father in Belsize Park. He took me to London Zoo and for walks in Hyde Park.

The summer of 1939 passed with my father anxiously waiting for news from my mother. I started to learn a little English, to add to the Czech and German that I already spoke. Barrage balloons were being tested – I have a clear mental image of large grey monsters on the ground, ready to be hoisted into the air to stop German bombers flying too low, so that the anti-aircraft fire could more easily get at them and the accuracy of their bombing would hopefully be reduced. I saw women from the ATS (Auxiliary Training Service, later the Women's Royal Army Corps) marching in Hyde Park, which made a big impression on me. In Prague, I had seen Nazi soldiers parading in formation in their jackboots. But to see women in their uniforms felt very different .

My father had a friend, a fellow Central European, who'd left Prague long before the war and had been able to take money out of the country with him. Foreigners were allowed by the British government to set up factories in Scotland or Northern Ireland, in areas of high unemployment. My father's friend had found a disused factory in Northern Ireland, where he set up a textile business, and he offered my father a job there if he got out. My father wrote to my mother and explained that if she could ever leave the country, we would move to

Cookstown. My mother said later that she had looked in an atlas and thought that meant we would be living in Australia, but it was a rather different Cookstown.

Eventually, my mother managed by one means or another to get an exit permit. She travelled by train, probably making the same journey as I had to Liverpool Street. My suspicion is that being Austrian, she had been friendly with an Austrian consul in Prague, who became a German official. He was probably responsible for securing her exit visa, just in time. She arrived in London on 31 August 1939, one day before Germany invaded Poland. Had she left a day later, she would almost certainly have been trapped.

Before she left, she had arranged for a removals company to collect our furniture and my father's beloved collection of old books and transport it all to England. Instead, they put it in storage in Prague, then demanded more money. But of course we didn't have any. The price had already been agreed, so it was very shabby of them. They essentially held our things to ransom. Then in 1940, the Nazis invaded and at some point took it all away. So we had very little from home – just a few clothes and very few photographs. My mother had a necklace, a reminder of more settled and comfortable times, though at some point she sold it. But we were together, and – physically at least – we were safe.

By this point, eight trains of unaccompanied, mainly Jewish children had arrived in London from Prague, thanks to Nicholas Winton and his network of helpers. The ninth, which had been scheduled to leave Prague perhaps forty-eight hours after my mother's train, never departed. On 3 September, Prime Minister Chamberlain announced that Britain was at war with Germany. Nicky said much later that he never found out what had happened to those children who were supposed to have been on the train. They disappeared, presumably to concentration camps.

II.

After my mother had safely arrived, we set off almost immediately for Northern Ireland.

Cookstown is about sixty miles from Belfast, in the middle of County Tyrone. It was a smallish town then, with the textile factory where my father was to start work about two miles outside. It was surrounded by fields, and cows would sometimes be driven down the road. It was all far more rural than what I was used to.

We rented a little cottage opposite a farmhouse. It was double-fronted, with a couple of bedrooms, and cost a pound a week – not an insignificant amount of money. It had a tiny backyard where we kept two chickens that supplied us with an egg a day – very important in those days of rationing. The number later grew to six, though they were rather intrepid birds and sometimes escaped, meaning we had to chase them across the fields.

I was enrolled in the local primary school, while my father started work and my mother struggled with a few words of English. There was one teacher for every two classes, teaching one while the other was given tasks. Another pupil was a refugee too – an Austrian Jewish boy called Alfred Posamentier, who was being looked after by the local doctor's family. He was a year ahead, but I got to know him quite well. Some evacuees from Belfast joined us at some point. The city was heavily bombed. We had no shelter in Cookstown, so when the air raid siren sounded, if we were at school, we simply sat under our desks.

There were also some Hungarian refugees who lived locally, so, although it was a small community, we weren't the only new arrivals in this uncertain time, when war had been declared but nothing much was happening yet. People were kind to us, but they were curious too. Although we were welcomed, I believe we were seen as quite eccentric. The school I went to was probably for Protestant children, although I wasn't aware of any sectarianism. My father was taken aback as people kept asking what his religion was. I'm not sure how much the answer – that he was Jewish agnostic – would have meant to them. Getting rather tired of the question, he once said that if anyone else asked him his religion, he would ask them for their income! The farmhouse across the road had no telephone, so sometimes people would call our phone and I would be sent over to find the farmer or whoever was wanted. That encouraged interaction with our neighbours.

As Czechs, we were classed as 'friendly aliens'. As opposed to 'enemy aliens' from Germany and Austria, and then Italy, who were considered potentially a threat by the British government and interned on the Isle of Man (of course, many refugees did get mixed into this and were sent to internment camps). This meant my father was subject to certain conditions, such as having to be indoors by 10 p.m., though that rule didn't apply to me as a young child. One day, when I was about seven, my father took me to the cinema, a twenty-minute walk from home. The film didn't finish until after my father had to leave to keep to his curfew, so he went home and left me to find my own way from the cinema. He explained the situation to the police officer as he walked past. It was a safe little town, so my late journey home was without risk. The blackout was in place but it wasn't very dark, so it was probably midsummer. My father laughed about it later – how I saw the end of the film, and he didn't!

My mother became very keen that we only spoke English outside of the house, and increasingly at home, too, instead of Czech. Typically for an immigrant, she was aware of our 'otherness' and probably wanted to draw as little attention to us as possible. Perhaps speaking English with me at home helped her gain confidence. Once the Nazis invaded France and the Low Countries in early May 1940, bypassing the much-lauded French defences and pushing the British army back to the coast with apparent ease, if one was heard speaking German anywhere in the British Isles it would have been met with alarmed looks, at the very minimum. Thanks to my mother's desire that I assimilate, I was definitely the only child at school who knew the words to more than one verse of the British national anthem.

Barely a year after my mother had made it to London and we had moved to Northern Ireland, my father suddenly died.

My father always went downstairs to listen to the 8 a.m. news. He tended to be overweight, and one morning he collapsed while he was listening to the wireless and had a heart attack. I saw him being helped upstairs. Later, he was carried to an ambulance and taken to hospital in Belfast. I never saw him again as he died that afternoon.

It was an awful shock. People rallied round and some friends suggested that I stayed with them for a day or two. They were very helpful and supportive. It was the first death I had encountered. I was seven and didn't know how to take it. It was too complicated and cataclysmic for me to comprehend. I was distraught and for several days dreamed that my father came back to life. It was very upsetting, but even more so for my mother.

It was incredibly tough for her to be in a foreign country, as a widow with a young son and limited English. She was left with no income and no idea what kind of future she could manage to have. Initially, she took in wives of British army officers as paying guests to make a little money. And for a time, she took a job in the factory where my father had worked.

But cycling there, out of town, in the wind and the snow, was too much for her. She had trained as a nurse and a dietician back home; like so many in these times, she found herself having to adapt to hugely different circumstances and manage as best she could, grieving, with no family around, worried about how to make ends meet.

People were kind to us. I desperately wanted a bicycle, but such things were very hard to come by in wartime, even if you had the money to buy one. One of the Hungarians we knew told me he would build me one out of spare parts. It took some time to amass all the bits he needed, and my anticipation grew and grew. When he said it was ready, I was very excited. I had learned to ride a bike before we left Prague, but I was around eight by this time, so someone helped me, and soon enough, I was off and away on two wheels.

After America entered the war at the end of 1941, some US regiments arrived in Cookstown, stationed mainly in a country house on the outskirts of the town. They built Nissen huts around the grounds. They gave out cookies to the local children – which was quite something at a time when so much was rationed – and I enjoyed eating peanut butter for the first time. They would throw out sweets onto the road for us to pick up, which was quite dangerous looking back on it now, but of course, we loved it.

My mother had an affair with an American colonel. He came from Iowa and he was a republican. Then his regiment was moved on, I think to Italy. The day they left, my mother was in tears. I can still see him kissing her goodbye, and then he got in his Jeep and off he went. They exchanged letters and she later learned that he had been injured, but that was the end of the relationship; she never saw him again. The Colonel asked me to write to his son, and we exchanged letters for a year or so, then stopped.

When I was ten, my mother was finding life in Cookstown too difficult and decided she could no longer manage in Northern Ireland. It was soon after the American colonel left. She needed a job and couldn't find one in Cookstown, and she had heard that the Czech government-in-exile had set up a school in Wales for children who had fled Czechoslovakia, which she wanted me to attend – the government-in-exile being the committee set up by President Edvard Beneš, who had resigned and fled to London in 1938, and which was regarded by the Allies as the legitimate Czech government. All school fees – for board and education – were covered by the government, which must have been a relief for my cash-strapped mother.

My mother had some Jewish friends from Austria who had a flat in Manchester's Whalley Range and were willing to take her in while she got settled. And so we packed up what belongings we had and again crossed the Irish sea. Another move, this time without my father. We travelled from Belfast to Liverpool by boat at night, which was presumably considered safe. There were rather frightening printed instructions telling us what to do in case we were attacked. As dawn broke, I could see smashed-up ships beached on the edge of the Mersey estuary that been hit by torpedoes or by bombs dropped on Liverpool's docks.

My mother found a job in Cheetham Hill scrubbing floors in a British Restaurant. These were canteens set up during the war to provide meals at reasonable prices for workers in factories and for people whose homes had been bombed or were otherwise in need. The hungry workers would say, 'All the way', meaning all five courses of starter, main, pudding, cheese and tea for a shilling and a penny. Later, she would secure a promotion and become a supervisor in another British Restaurant in Gorton.

When we first arrived in Manchester from Northern Ireland, I was a very naive little boy. One day, my mother asked me to meet her on a street corner in Moss Side. When I arrived, I saw a sign that said, 'No waiting'. Not realising it did not apply to pedestrians, I walked purposefully backwards and forwards until she arrived.

Soon afterwards, my mother once again put me on a train and waved me off. This time I was ten and headed to boarding school, again in a new place that was unknown to me. Here, at least, there would be children with whom I shared a first language, and who had been through similar experiences to me. But as I said goodbye to my mother, that was little consolation. Instead, I was consumed by anxiety that I would lose her somehow. She was sleeping on her friends' sofa and we had nowhere to call home. I was so worried that if she went somewhere else, if a letter from her went astray and I didn't receive it, I would never be able to find her again. Since we had left Prague, there hadn't been anywhere that represented home. I felt I didn't belong anywhere, and I was terrified by the thought that the last connection I had – that vital link to my remaining parent – could be severed by something as simple as misdirected mail. I still remember that feeling very acutely, even now. I believe that these early experiences of feeling rootless, adrift, and the memories of boarding trains alone had a profound influence on me. All through my life I have had a strong dislike of being seen off on a journey, but have always loved being met when I arrived back.

I went first to Malpas in Cheshire, the Czech school for primary age pupils, and then to the Abernant Lake Hotel in Llanwrtyd Wells in Breconshire, which had been taken over by the Czech Government in 1943 to educate secondary school-age pupils. Many had come on the Kindertransports like I had; others were the children of Czech soldiers and airmen who were serving with the British, or of civil servants and officials working with the exiled government. Many but not all of the 140 pupils were Jewish. The aim was to ensure we didn't forget our Czech language or culture, in the hope that, at the end of the war, we would be able to return to our homeland.

I wasn't conscious of losing my mother tongue, although we rarely spoke it at home by this point, my mother being so keen that we were only overheard speaking in English. Lessons at the school were partly in English and partly in Czech. I spoke quite good English by then; in fact, a bus conductor in Manchester thought I was Irish, so I must have picked up a little of the accent. He was very surprised to be told I was from Czechoslovakia.

Being one of the youngest at the secondary school, I found everything bewildering and remained extremely anxious. It was a welcoming environment, and the food was pretty good. It was on the edge of a little village with a stream and lovely grounds, and we would enjoy a walk into the village. We lived in dormitories with eight bunk beds. Somehow, although I was generally an insecure child who lacked confidence, I became the storyteller of the dorm every night when the lights were out. I found it easy to make up stories about detectives off the top of my head. It was useful because if I was bullied I could threaten not to tell a story – though in general the children got along. We were all in the same boat, all away from our parents, even if they had fled to England. But despite this, it was a cheerful place. I might have enjoyed school life more had I been older and feeling more secure.

The school was in effect a showpiece for the Czech government-in-exile, so from time to time we received eminent visitors. The uniforms of the senior officers of the Czech army or air force reminded us of the war going on – in the Welsh hills we felt very cut off from outside events. However, one day an RAF plane crashed into the mountains nearby and we later learned that the crew were all killed. We could see the smoke from the wreckage; it was very dramatic and quite frightening.

After sleeping on floors and sofas of friends from Austria, eventually my mother found a bedsit in Whalley Range, which became my home during the school holidays. It was small and cramped and temporary-feeling, but at least I knew where she was while I was at school. When I was there, my mother used to send me to the local grocer at the edge of Moss Side with the ration books. Apart from the two ounces a week or so of butter and other items, which were a fixed ration, there was also a points system, where one could choose among different products such as sardines, cereals and baked beans. My job was to use our points to best advantage, and I took the responsibility very seriously.

Many years after the war, school reunions were organised, and I attended a few, where I learned that my former school companions were dispersed all over the world. Which is perhaps unsurprising when you think how many would have discovered, at the war's end, that they had been left without family and would have to make their own way. Some did go back to Prague. One reached a senior position in the State Department in Washington DC, while others went to Australia and Israel. I'm still in touch with a couple of former school friends from those days in Wales.

Another of my friends at the Czech school was Tommy Freund, whose father was an active Communist and worked on the *Daily Worker* during the war. Tommy returned to

Prague with his father. Then came the notorious antisemitic show trials, in this case the Slánský trial in 1952, and his father was one of those accused of plotting against the Communist government. Tommy was by then a student in East Berlin and apparently was coerced into denouncing his father as a 'Western agent'. Most of the defendants were executed, including Tommy's father. It was shocking to read about this and to realise what was happening to one of my former school friends. He and I were both enthusiastic stamp collectors, like many children in those days, and he was always excessively keen to acquire some of my Russian stamps. I understand that Tommy, who had already changed his name from Freund to Frejka, eventually left Czechoslovakia, became a professor in the United States and changed his name yet again.

I was twelve when the war ended. People were singing and dancing in the streets on VE day. I was in Manchester, and I felt the sense of the enormity, but also the unreality, of the occasion.

As joyful as it was, the end of the war meant the closure of the Czech school. I would have to move again and fit in with a whole new set of schoolmates. Some of my fellow pupils, Jewish children who had also arrived unaccompanied on the Kindertransports, were waiting to learn the fate of those relatives they had left behind. News often came slowly at the time as camps were liberated and family members desperately tried to hear word of one another. My mother, too, was hoping for word of friends and my father's family, who had remained in Prague.

In September 1945, my mother sent me to a small school in Kent so that I would get used to the English school system. She was determined to get me into a good school and would have wanted me to be closer to home. I had not taken the eleven plus exam, but somehow was accepted into Cheadle Hulme school, in Greater Manchester, which was then a grammar school. My English was not bad, and my maths was good. They must have taken pity on me.

By that time, my mother had progressed from working in the British Restaurant to become a more senior person in the schools' meals service, first in Manchester and later in Blackburn, where she worked as a deputy school meals' organiser. She would have to decide our future – whether to try to return to Prague or stay and continue the fragile life she had worked to build for us in Britain.

III.

Churchill wanted to wait until the end of the war in Asia before calling a general election, but the Labour Party was determined to go to the country as soon as possible after victory in Europe was declared. They won out, and on 15 June 1945, Churchill was forced to ask King George to dissolve Parliament.

I was terribly excited by the whole thing. Although I wasn't yet thirteen, I quickly became passionately interested in politics. Never having known such a thing as an election, I walked around Manchester looking at the campaign posters that suddenly appeared everywhere. The city had sustained much damage, and there were bomb sites everywhere. But that summer, hundreds of small purple flowers grew up through the rubble.

All the parties made much use of posters in those days, what with paper for leafletting being in short supply and television not yet having arrived. One announced that Captain Hugh Delargy, your Labour candidate, will address voters on his return from the Western Front, which seemed very impressive. While the Conservatives led with slogans like 'Confirm your confidence in Churchill' and 'Let him finish the job', the Labour campaign spoke of nationalisation of the country's resources such as coal, free universal healthcare and better housing for all. The end of the war saw collective trauma in a country scarred by bomb damage and loss of life. So the opportunity to look forward and the possibility of building something new was irresistible to many.

It's hard to say exactly where my interest in politics originated. My mother was not any more politically engaged than the average person at the time. I had, of course, learned about what the Nazis had done. I had cried when I watched a newsreel about the Lidice massacre with my mother in 1942, which told how all the men in a Czech village had been lined up and shot by the Nazis in retaliation for two Czech resistance fighters blowing up General Heydrich's car in Prague. Foreign secretary Antony Eden confirmed in the House of Commons in December that year that Jews in Nazi camps were being put to death. And in the spring of 1945, photographs and accounts started to come from Allied armies arriving at concentration camps. The scale of the atrocities was almost impossible to take in, even from a distance. But I believed that if evil people could do such terrible things, they could be countered by others doing something good. I wanted to know more about politics to understand events in my early life and make sense of it all somehow.

Polling began at the beginning of July, but the count didn't take place until three weeks later, to allow time for ballot papers from service personnel stationed in the Far East to come in. I followed the campaigning avidly and read about the candidates in the *Manchester Guardian*. While I didn't know enough to understand the ins and outs of the party's manifestos, the idea that you could build a society that was fairer for everyone, and that politics was the thing that could make that happen, was very appealing. I quickly decided that I wanted the Labour Party and its leader, Clement Attlee, to win.

On the day that the election results were due to come out my mother and I were on holiday in St Annes, near Blackpool, staying at a boarding house. In the absence of television, the BBC would broadcast the results from the town square as they came in. I was sent to bring back the latest news, and I gladly ran over there. On my return, I announced with pride to the other boarding house guests that, at that time, Labour was on something like 120 seats and the Tories on 30. As I did, I heard a voice say in a very posh accent, 'Oh my God, it's the end of England.' That convinced me that I was right to support Labour.

Churchill had miscalculated. There had not been a general election for ten years at this point, but many senior Labour politicians had served in the wartime coalition government and were well known and respected by the electorate. Though some, like my fellow boarding house guest, were suspicious of the radical social change promised by the Labour Party, the general mood in the country was of optimism, almost entirely free of the cynicism that is so prevalent these days.

I watched with enthusiasm as the Labour government began to implement its programme. I saw cinema newsreels of the miners celebrating at the pitheads on the day the mines were nationalised – 1 January 1947. For Christmas 1947, my mother and I travelled to London to see some distant relatives. The railways were due to be nationalised the following morning. We returned to Blackburn on New Year's Eve and found ourselves in the waiting room at Preston station on a cold, snowy evening with no heating and no sign of our connecting train. One person in the waiting room proclaimed that from tomorrow morning, we could blame the government!

The move towards nationalisation coincided with my developing an irreverent streak. A few months later, I was quite ill with recurring trouble with my ears and was admitted to Stockport Royal Infirmary. I was there on the very day the National Health Service began – 5 July 1948 – the only child in the ward. In those days healthcare was very formal. When the consultant, the matron and their teams did the ward round, patients didn't exactly stand to attention, but you felt almost as though you had to lie to attention in bed. The doctors expected deference, and, in addition, it was an era in which, as a child, one did not speak unless one was spoken to.

A consultant examined me and was about to walk on with his team when I said, 'Excuse me, may I ask you a question . . . ? Are we having a party today?' The consultant was nonplussed. With glee, I said, 'Well, the hospital's ours, and we should celebrate.' I got a disapproving look and no answer to my question. The important people moved on, and I spent the day repeating to the other patients in the ward what had happened. It was a useful distraction from my illness and the general boredom of having to be in hospital.

Though my interest in politics was growing, I knew almost no one with any direct connections to a political party. The exception was my mother's boss at the school meals' service in Blackburn. I believe her name was Miss Jowett. She was a staunch Labour supporter and knew local party figures. She and I would talk about politics when I met my mother after work during the school holidays. I didn't know anyone else who was interested in politics in this way, and these conversations had a strong influence on me.

Throughout my teens, I remained passionately interested in politics, even though none of my contemporaries showed any interest. I had learned the hard way that we needed to use politics for better and worthier ends. It is a belief that has never left me.

In 1947, my mother had her first post-war opportunity to visit Prague. Europe was in turmoil for a long time after the end of the war – infrastructure destroyed, food shortages, different occupying armies. It was very difficult for the displaced millions to know what to do. She eventually booked a flight and returned that summer, which was quite a brave thing for her to do. There was no question of me going with her, so she arranged for me to stay with the family of a boy I was at school with in Cheadle Hulme in their home near Birmingham. While my mother looked for remnants of our old life and tried to find the people we used to know, my schoolfriend and I spent long, hot days down at the mainline railway tracks watching the trains and 'collecting' their numbers as they went past. This sort of trainspotting was popular among boys at the time, although I found it dull. Luckily, I had a book to read.

My mother could recall a 'golden age' in Prague that didn't exist for me. It is painful to imagine her feelings as she discovered that our family and friends had either fled the country to escape the Nazis or had ended up in the camps. Some who had survived the camps had left Czechoslovakia by the time of my mother's visit. She realised we knew no one in the city, which was now typical for Jewish families. Edvard Beneš had been restored as president but was under increasing pressure from the Soviets; indeed, the following year, the Communists would take power. After we left, our flat had been taken over by another family and housing in general was in short supply. There were no jobs to be had. It was clear to her that without somewhere for us to live and a way for her to earn money, we could not return. It is a typical situation for refugees to find themselves in. A crisis may pass, but for them, there is often no way back. We didn't discuss her visit much when she returned, though over the years she told me what she had seen and learned about events after we left.

We stayed in Lancashire. When her boss resigned, my mother filled in as the school meals' organiser for six months. She applied for the official vacancy, but no one was appointed. She kept on doing the job, and applied again, but was once more turned down for the role she was already performing, perfectly competently. It was hard to account for it, until one day, she overheard one of the councillors from the selection panel saying, 'We are not giving a job to that bloody foreigner.' She was very upset. Looking back, I did not understand how this discrimination would have affected her, and sadly I was not mature enough to give her more support. She applied for many jobs and did eventually get one, still as a school meals' organiser, on the Isle of Wight.

Once again, she packed up her small number of belongings, this time moving south. Initially, she rented two rooms in a semi-detached house in Carisbrooke, near the castle. Later, she rented a small flat in Cowes. It was the first time since Prague that she and I had lived in a proper home.

Fleeing Prague had caused us to lose almost everything of the life we'd had. We had left behind our home, almost all our possessions and contact with our extended family and friends. Only a handful of photos came with us on our separate journeys to the UK, very little else. My strongest feelings from my formative years were that there was nowhere that I could identify as home. And yet, crucially, we had hope. What we had lost was replaced by the different life we were able to forge. I can see now that those early experiences must have influenced many of my later decisions, and my motivation for going into public service. Above all, I have always wanted to give similar hope to people who like me had fled their homes.

I was by now at the end of my secondary schooling and decided that I wanted to go to university to study government. I was still fascinated by politics, but had no knowledge of how one actually got a job in that field, and certainly not how you might become an MP. I had read some of the writings of political theorist and socialist Harold Laski, who taught at the London School of Economics, and so I applied there and was accepted. Sadly, Laski died before I took up my place, but I remained excited at the prospect of living in London and becoming an undergraduate.

In order to get a university grant I was interviewed by a panel from the county council. My mother's boss was on it – she was chair of the council and had been a Liberal candidate. She was an intelligent, inspiring person who took three of us local boys under her wing and encouraged us. It was invaluable to have an adult advise me in this way. She once said to me, 'You don't want to spend your life making rich men richer,' something that very much stayed with me.

During the interview, I responded to mostly Conservative and Liberal councillors in a way that clearly showed my nascent political inclinations. One of them said, 'Well, we can see which way this young man is going.' They gave me the grant anyway.

*

In 1951, in the summer before I went to university, my friend Michael and I decided we would take a cycling trip to Vienna. Cycling was all the rage, and by now it was possible to travel around much of Western Europe, although we still needed a permit from the Soviets to enter one zone of Austria.

I set off from the Isle of Wight and Michael rode down from Sheffield. We met at Dover and took the ferry across the Channel – there were hundreds of other cyclists. Petrol rationing had ended the year before but few people owned cars. We disembarked at Calais, and then there we were in France, our wheels going bump, bump, bump over the cobbles, little Union Jacks stuck to our bike frames.

We had very little money and we got incredibly hungry as we pedalled our basic three-speed bikes across Europe. We lived largely off bread as it was cheap, and stayed in youth hostels. Once we slept in a barn.

At school, we'd had a French *assistante* who was from Sedan, in the Ardennes, by the Belgian border. She had said that we could visit if we were ever passing through, so without any warning we called in. She was away but her family gave us a warm welcome.

As we cycled along the French–Belgian border, we saw First World War cemeteries that stretched for miles, row upon row of graves blurring together until they almost seemed like an optical illusion. I'd had no idea about the cemeteries' scale, and found it both moving and terrifying.

Germany was very economically depressed, and everywhere

we went on the roads we saw people hitchhiking, travelling in search of work. It felt odd to speak German, which I had to do frequently because we often had to ask for directions. My German was still fairly good. We encountered no other foreigners and were greeted with curiosity and some bemusement. It was even odder to meet former Nazi soldiers. One day, we met two men who had served with the German army on the Eastern Front. They had briefly been captured by the Russians, but then the Germans had counterattacked and freed them. They would have been unlikely to survive as prisoners of war.

Another couple of men we met rolled up their sleeves to show us their tattoos, which meant they had been members of the SS. They told us that when captured by the British they would get a violent smack to the head when these identifying tattoos were spotted. Nevertheless, they were friendly to us and eager to talk about England.

In Austria, we met up with my mother's brothers and her sister. Her sister-in-law rented a house in a beautiful place in the mountains where we stayed along with my cousins. We talked a little about what had happened to them in Austria during the war. It sounded like they'd had it very hard. They were very kind to me, and it was a strange but pleasant feeling to have a sense of family. I was used to it being just my mum and me.

We returned home after six weeks – no doubt very fit after covering all those miles, but somewhat lean on account of our rather meagre diet. I lost touch with Michael after our trip, which I regret. I was not very good at staying in touch with people then; it didn't occur to me that it was something I should do. A result of my rather transient life up to that point.

IV.

'You don't have to like it, just learn to drink it' was the sage advice of a slightly older, more worldly student. I was sitting doubtfully in front of a pint of beer in a pub near Passfield Hall, the Georgian townhouse halls of residence in which I had been allocated a room. It proved to be useful tip, although I did come to like beer eventually.

I was in my first few weeks of university, and the Conservatives had just won the general election. The exhilaration of the Labour government had fallen by the wayside. Churchill was once again prime minister. For some, that would have felt reassuring; for the rest of us, it was like going back in time. But, at the very least, politics was in the air and there were plenty of interesting conversations to have. I found my lectures intellectually exciting, helped by the presence of quite a lot of older undergraduates who had served in the armed forces and therefore brought a different perspective to that usually offered by callow eighteen- or nineteen-year-old students.

The general election of 1951 also gave me my first experience of canvassing. I volunteered to go out with members of the local Labour Party around Holborn and St Pancras. I was so keen that they probably thought I was a little odd. The area was largely tenements then, rather than the expensive flats and office blocks that are there now. I enjoyed canvassing immensely. Although I was not a confident young man, somehow I was happy to knock on doors to ask people how they planned to vote. When speaking to them about issues that affected all of our lives and listening to what they had to say, I felt I was really taking part in politics. It was a contrast to the theory and debate of my university lectures. It was around this time that I joined the Labour Party.

On the whole, I was very happy at university. I could have perhaps done with a little more tuition, as LSE left us to our own devices. And for my part, I could have worked harder. I didn't have much money, but that didn't matter. I had learned to budget quickly after one afternoon when I had taken a young woman to a Lyon's Corner House for tea only to realise I had spent almost all of what remained of my grant for the term. University accommodation was rather sparse and would perhaps have proved something of an adjustment for students from more stable, solidly middle-class lifestyles, but accustomed as I had been to moving around and living between bedsitters and boarding school, it was no trouble.

In 1954 I graduated with a BSc in government and off I went to do my national service, as almost all young men had to at that time. It was boring and not at all enjoyable, though there was a sense of camaraderie. I spent some time stationed near Paris, which made things more lively.

My first job after leaving the army was as a supply teacher. You didn't need a formal qualification to do that in those days. I didn't see myself as a teacher, but it was a job, and I hoped it might be interesting. I was offered a role at a school in Pitfield Street, in the borough of Hackney. The person who offered it to me to sounded somewhat dubious. I asked what the problem was, and they asked if I was familiar with the area. I said I wasn't, as I had been away with the army, and they told me that the school had something of a reputation, and that the teachers would huddle together to walk home out of fear of the pupils. I thought, oh dear, this could be rather *too* interesting.

As is so often the case, the reality was not as bad as the rumours had it. Some of the children struggled academically and seemed to have been let down by the system. There was one bright kid who could barely read; I had to give him extra lessons during lunch hour. The main problem wasn't the pupils, it was that I had no idea how to teach. I quickly learned that I had to have everything well planned – if I paused or hesitated, I would lose control of the class. This was useful preparation for later experiences speaking in the House of Commons. It was utterly exhausting – I would often get home to my bedsit and fall asleep while listening to the six o'clock news on the radio, sometimes jerking awake at 9 p.m.

In those days, one signed on at the local Labour Exchange when seeking work; they became Jobcentres in 1973. Through the Labour Exchange, I had applied for a job with an advertising agency, J. Walter Thompson, although I didn't expect to hear anything. But suddenly one day, I got a call at school to tell me I should go for an interview immediately. I had just come back from taking the kids to play football, so I was covered in mud and looking fairly scruffy. But off I went, and they offered me the job, doing marketing and market research.

I started off at the offices in Berkeley Square in Mayfair. It was very smart and the sort of place where you could expect to be asked what school you went to. I don't know what my new colleagues made of my answer: 'the school of the Czech government-in-exile'. It was my first experience of the public school world and I found it strange. They were a friendly enough bunch, though, and there were plenty of after-work trips to the pub.

All the same, I didn't enjoy it. I felt myself to be philosophically opposed to advertising. Even after I was moved to the Ealing office where the focus was on market research, I was the only left-wing person there. The work could be intellectually stimulating, but in the end I was making rich men richer, just as my mother's boss had cautioned me against. I nearly left quite early on, but then there came to be a reason for me to stay.

My mother had settled on the Isle of Wight and met some

very nice people. She was happy on the island, and loved her seafront flat in Cowes. It had been a very nice place for me to go back to during university holidays. I used to cycle round the island, and very occasionally went sailing.

But then she was diagnosed with leukaemia. I asked the consultant how long she had, and he said five years, which proved to be right. She wanted me to be settled, following the upheaval of my childhood and our worries about money. She found it reassuring to know that I had a reasonably well-paid, secure job, and I didn't like to tell her I was not enjoying it. And so I stuck out the marketing role.

When I was working in London in the mid-fifties I had a good friend called Gerald. One day, he suggested that we visit the woman he was engaged to, who'd had a very nice flat in Eccleston Square loaned to her. Importantly for us, that meant she had access to the private tennis court in the square. I thought this sounded like a good idea, so off we went.

Gerald's fiancée was sharing the flat with a very pretty young woman called Ann. She had studied ballet quite seriously in her youth but had turned down an audition for a prestigious dance company because her mother hadn't thought that sort of life suitable for her. She had studied modern languages at university instead, and was working as a secondary school teacher. We didn't talk much on that first meeting, but before long, we had hit it off. We were married on 24 October 1959.

It was a quiet ceremony at the Westminster Register Office in Caxton Hall. My mother was too ill to attend, but she was able to come to the wedding reception that Ann's parents put on for us at the house near Westerham in Kent.

My mother died the following year. She was only in her mid-fifties. It was very sad. She had worked so hard to keep us going after my father had died, scrubbing floors and striving for better jobs, all of which were still worse than those her qualifications should have allowed. Despite her lack of fluency in English – she never lost her strong accent – she made sure I got the best education she could manage. Looking back now, I see how tough and resourceful her circumstances required her to be.

When she died I was twenty-seven. I was far from being a child, but having lost both my parents, and knowing no other family, I felt quite alone.

When my mother was alive, she hadn't wanted me to visit Prague. The Communists were in power and she was afraid I would be forced to do national service if I returned. I don't know how big this risk actually was, but it worried her deeply, so I didn't go. I had not seen the city or country of my birth since I was six years old.

After she died, I decided to go with Ann. Now, without siblings or parents, I was looking for some connection. Rationally, I knew that virtually all of my mother and father's Jewish friends in the city had either ended up in the camps or fled the country. Nevertheless, Ann and I drove there in our old banger of a car during her school holidays.

Seeing Prague again for the first time since I left in 1939 was a deeply emotional experience. The sensation of half-remembering places was strange, as was the sense that I was now a foreigner there. The Communist regime was strict, but it allowed privileges for foreigners that were not accessible to local Czech people. We didn't have a hotel booking, so we went to the tourist information centre, which was chaos – it seemed like there were hundreds of Czechs at the desk all trying to get attention. But with my British passport, I was immediately directed to a small, separate counter and attended. They sent us to a little hotel which also catered for the Russian delegation to Prague, so it was a cut above others. Initially, they treated us well because they thought we were Russian. They were even more welcoming when they discovered we weren't.

In a supposedly socialist country, I was shocked to discover there were special shops, *tuzek*, that stocked a wide range of goods unobtainable elsewhere and served only senior Communist Party members and foreigners with hard currency. One day, we met a Czech couple and started to talk with them. He was a coal miner from northern Czechoslovakia. We offered to take them out to a restaurant. When we arrived, they went ahead of us to the door and were told there were no places. I moved forward and, of course, was told there was a table for four, given I was a foreigner. My coal-miner friend and his wife were embarrassed to be in a restaurant that seemed to have mostly senior party members as customers. My Czech wasn't good enough to ease the situation.

I went to look at where we had lived on Holečkova in Smíchov. The flat numbers seemed to have changed since the war and I didn't know which had been ours. It was moving to see where I had grown up before I fled. In fact, many parts of Prague still had memories for me, including Wenceslas Square, near where my father's cousins had lived.

Leaving Prague behind, Ann and I travelled on to Austria, where we met a friend of my parents. She and her husband had been taken to the camps, where he died. She left the room where we were talking and returned with a plate. On it was a picture of a large house outside Prague, among the pine forests, which she and her husband used to rent. They would often invite friends to stay, and I remembered it. It was in a beautiful spot, but I knew that as a child I had found the pine forest dark and frightening, especially when sent to collect kindling for the fire. Around the outside of the plate were the twenty-three or so names of people who had stayed there in the summer of 1938. One by one, she went through them all. Only she, one other person and I were alive.

Part Two

MEMBER OF PARLIAMENT

I.

I never believed I could become an MP. The enthusiasm for politics that I'd felt in 1945, seeing posters around Manchester promising a fairer society for all, had not dimmed, though it had perhaps matured. I enjoyed being part of the local Labour Party in Paddington, where we lived, but unlike many of those I encountered, I had not grown up in a household steeped in left-wing politics. I envied those who could draw on family traditions and conversations at home. I felt like an outsider in the wider Labour movement.

The general election of 1964 returned a Labour government with a majority of four. Harold Wilson went to the country again in 1966, resulting in a greater majority. Unemployment was low, but there was a sense that Britain was lagging behind some of our European neighbours in terms of the modernisation of industry and financial systems. But there was once again a feeling of change and possibility in the air, albeit more muted or circumspect than in the years immediately following the war.

Wilson himself had come from a political family and had studied at Oxford. His Home Secretary was Roy Jenkins, whose father had been a miner, an official in the National Union of Mineworkers and later an MP. Jenkins had been to Oxford too. I had not been to Oxbridge nor worked down a mine. For a time, I thought it would be somehow inappropriate for someone who was born in another country, who had been a refugee, and who did not come from a political family, to set their sights on becoming a member of Parliament.

However, my ambition remained to get involved in politics. I was still working in marketing and market research, and had begun to think I should get out of advertising now or I never would. Ann knew that I disliked the job, and she was supportive when I decided to leave, even though it meant taking a rather large pay cut. Which was no minor decision as we had two small children by then.

I thought the civil service might be the thing, and so I applied and was accepted into the fast-track scheme. I was excited by the prospect of doing something more aligned with my interests. Some of the work was interesting – looking after hospitals in East Anglia was an instructive lesson in how local health services worked. But I was placed under an assistant secretary who was on his way to retirement and was not demanding enough. I was hoping to be challenged and pushed, but it was all very slow and uninspiring. So eventually I returned to work in market research.

I next set my sights on becoming a local councillor. But 1968 saw large Labour losses in the London councils, so there were no vacancies locally. Then an interesting opportunity came up. The party was looking for candidates to contest the seat of Cities of London and Westminster in the 1970 general election. It was a fascinating constituency, going all the way from the Royal Albert Hall in the west to some old tenement blocks in Stepney, and taking in the financial district. It had been a Conservative stronghold since its creation in 1950, and was not seen as a winnable seat. I spoke to a number of people I respected, including an MP, and was convinced to throw my hat into the ring. It would serve as an important test for me and potentially a step on the ladder. If one had ambitions to become an MP, it was something of a rite of passage to fight an election for a Tory safe seat. So I put myself forward and – somewhat to my surprise – I was selected.

My opponent was Christopher Tugendhat, who was born in Austria. The newspapers never picked up on the fact that the seat at the political and financial heart of the Empire was being contested by refugees from Prague and Vienna, respectively.

One novel experience I had was to canvass the staff at Buckingham Palace. I phoned up and was given an appointment. When I arrived, I received an apology for having been asked to appear at the servants' entrance. I was assured that all the staff had postal votes, as the court was moving to Windsor the following Monday. I had an interesting chat with the half-dozen or so staff who turned up in response to information on their noticeboard. What struck me most was that for the staff, the palace was their whole life. The outside world hardly impinged on their day-to-day. I also canvassed in Soho and Covent Garden, and knocked on the door of my former politics professor at LSE, Michael Oakeshott. He told me he didn't vote, using the old cliché: 'Because it only encourages them!'

On election day I was featured on the cover of the *Guardian*, canvassing outside the Houses of Parliament, which was quite fun. While most of the election results were counted on Thursday night, the Westminster constituency counted the votes on Friday morning, so I had to wait until then to have it confirmed that I had lost. I wasn't surprised, but what was much worse was that Labour had lost the election overall, despite the opinion polls having predicted a comfortable Labour victory. Ted Heath was to be the next prime minister. It was a very gloomy day.

Some months later, I was introduced to Harold and Mary Wilson. Harold Wilson had remained as the leader of the Labour Party in opposition. I explained that I had been the Labour candidate for the constituency that included 10 Downing Street, and I said to Harold, 'And so you voted for me.' To which Mary interjected, 'How do you know?' I had a laugh at that.

*

The following year, I was selected as the candidate for the Westbourne ward on Westminster City Council. Labour had been almost wiped out in the 1968 local elections, so we were pleased to regain eighteen seats in total, including mine. Thus began a most exciting period in my life, my first opportunity to be involved in serious politics and to influence decisions that affect people's lives.

On one occasion, while canvassing for my council seat, I arrived at a house that had been divided into flats. I had the list of registered voters but no flat numbers. There were no names on the bells and some of them weren't even working. I pressed one at random, and a mother and small child appeared at the door. I tried to discover their names before asking how they intended to vote, but the mother simply shut the door. Just as I was about to ring the next bell, the door opened again, and the mother said to the enquiring child: 'There's nothing to see, it's only a politician.' I left a sadder and wiser person. In later years, I would tell this story at Labour Party meetings to illustrate the point that if people thought we were 'just' politicians, we had failed.

One difficulty for me was that councillors – then, as now – didn't get paid. Nowadays, councillors have a more reasonable annual allowance, but at that time, they received only an expense payment for attending each meeting. It was a derisory sum – from memory: around £5 for a committee meeting and £7 for a council meeting. So, unless you were lucky enough to have some private income, you had to work. Despite the very useful skills one learns, employers weren't always keen to have councillors on their staff, as they did not appreciate how we needed to juggle our time and would rather we were single-minded about our work.

Politics was of much more importance to me than my job, but of course I needed to earn money. The two often clashed. On one occasion I was due to open a debate at Westminster City Council when my employer insisted that I travel abroad to deliver a market research presentation to a client. Clashes kept arising and I thought that the situation couldn't go on. If I was to make a success of being a councillor, if there was any chance that it would lead on to something else for me, then I would have to get a job that was more compatible with my political interests.

One was advertised with the London Borough of Lewisham in its central policy unit. The main problem at the job interview was explaining why I was willing to take a nearly 40 per cent salary cut. I also had to explain this to Ann, of course, who fortunately was as supportive as ever. I was appointed by Lewisham Council, and belts were tightened accordingly at home. Looking back, that time – with the children at primary school, Anne back working as a teacher, my job with Lewisham and being a councillor, along with social and family life – was extraordinarily busy and often quite exhausting. And yet, admittedly at a distance of years, we both remember it as very happy.

My main areas of work for Lewisham Council were on the

race relations working party and on care for the elderly, both social support for those discharged from hospital and social care more widely. Later, I helped set up a women's rights working party to examine who the council was employing and the differences in pay and promotions. The race relations working party was interesting and rewarding, as it was an effective committee that attracted positive attention from other councils and some universities.

One important conference on race relations was held in the council chamber in Lewisham. The National Front heard about it and began handing out leaflets outside, opposing the council's policies. I went out to see what was going on and found an NF person with about a hundred leaflets near the door. I asked if I could see one. He looked pleased and surprised by my interest. I then asked if I could have some more and grabbed the lot from him. They went straight in the bin.

Between Lewisham and being a councillor on Westminster City Council, work was extraordinarily varied. As a councillor, I often visited people at home who had asked me to see them about a particular problem. Two elderly women had been in touch as they wanted help filling in a council form. I arrived at the basement flat they shared in the late afternoon, and it was getting dark. They showed me into the kitchen, but it was impossible to see the form as there was no light. They explained they could not climb up to put in a new light bulb, and so for several months, they had prepared food and cooked only in daylight. They did have a new bulb, though, which I was able to fit for them in a matter of seconds. When I asked why they hadn't asked a neighbour for help, they said they were too embarrassed. This was a very sad example of how elderly people can be terribly isolated and suffer in silence for want of a tiny piece of help.

Of course, not all issues were so easy to solve. At Westminster, I became the Labour lead on the Social Services Committee at a time when we were very concerned about policies for children in care. The council was building children's homes at considerable cost. One Tory councillor huffed that it would be cheaper to send the children to Eton and put them in the Dorchester hotel for holidays. I had some friends working for social services in other London boroughs, with whom I was able to discuss the complicated situation. They persuaded me that keeping children in institutions should be avoided, if possible. A good foster family could provide the love and care that institutions found it hard to offer. The trouble was that there weren't all that many foster parents in our council area. We researched what was stopping more potential foster parents from coming forward, and discovered that the cost of caring for a child exceeded what Westminster Council was offering foster families. We persuaded the council that while fostering should never be a for-profit activity, more parents might volunteer if they had greater financial support and weren't left out of pocket. The policy was adopted and more foster parents were recruited. On one occasion, the Lord Mayor invited foster parents and children to a celebration at City Hall. It was a lovely day, and the children were very impressed to see the mayor wearing his ceremonial robes.

Housing was, as ever, an important topic. Something like 40 per cent of people in London lived in a house or flat that was owned by the council in those days. Then, in August 1972, Ugandan dictator Idi Amin expelled the Asian population from the country, giving them ninety days to leave. Uganda had been a British colony until 1962. After independence, Asian minorities – many of whom had been encouraged to migrate there by the British colonial authorities – were allowed to retain their UK citizenship if they so chose. Consequently, a large number held British passports and therefore had the legal right to come to the UK, which many of course did, having had their property seized in Uganda and often their possessions stolen by the army. Others who lacked this documentation were made stateless. Either way, these people had no choice but to leave their homes.

On a national level, it caused consternation in some quarters, and several newspapers questioned their right to come to the UK at all, despite the fact they were passport holders. But the evacuation flights had to go ahead, and these people needed somewhere to live. The government appealed to local authorities to provide some of the refugees with housing. The proposition before the council was that we should put fifty Ugandan Asian families at the top of our council housing list. This split both the Labour and Conservative groups on the council. As someone who had himself been a refugee, I could perhaps appreciate better than most what these people were going through, though I was fully aware of the situation's complexity. Within the council's Labour group, there was a strong concern that we were depriving families already on the waiting list of the chance of decent housing. On the other hand, there was a feeling that we should help victims of repression, who after all, had British passports.

In the end, the council voted to give fifty flats to Ugandan Asian families, but there was a lot of ill feeling. I supported the allocation, but it was disconcerting that most of the working-class Labour councillors took a different view. The resettlement programme was done with relative speed and was an overall success, with many finding jobs quickly and avoiding the limbo that affects refugees today.

Many of those who came became victims of racism stirred by the National Front. The parents of former Home Secretary Priti Patel fled to the UK from Uganda in the 1960s and some of her family members benefitted from the support given to the Ugandan Asians – something she seemed to have forgotten when in office. Thankfully, her plan to send some of Britain's current refugees in the opposite direction to Rwanda, Uganda's neighbour, never came to fruition. Her motto seemed to be: 'I'll pull up the drawbridge now that I am inside.'

Tensions between the community and police in London were on the rise, and I soon had a brush with the justice system which illuminated them. Shortly after being elected to Westminster

City Council, I attended an appointment with the Notting Hill People's Association to discuss nursery support for the under-fives, a community organisation set up in the late 1960s to unite various activist groups in west London. While we were chatting, someone rushed in to say there was trouble at the Metro. The Metro Club was a youth club and community centre with an Afro-Caribbean membership. We all decided to go and investigate. Relations between the police and the local Notting Hill black community were then strained to the point where I imagined that having an independent observer from the council present might be useful.

The problem apparently was that one of the youngsters in the club had robbed a bus conductor of some money, then had entered the club and locked the doors. Unfortunately, the police commander at Harrow Road police station was away on leave, and the person who was standing in for him had no idea how to handle local sensitivities regarding the Metro. He seemed to have decided to treat the problem as a kind of terrorist incident. It was a tense situation, with police cars and officers very much in evidence.

I positioned myself near the door of the club, which was still locked. It was a miserable, wet evening, and several times the police half-charged to move us away. It got later and later, but I couldn't leave, as I had been asked to stay. Then at about 1 a.m. an agreement was reached and the youngsters, dozens of them, streamed out of the club. Through the parked cars and trees, I could see that there was some activity somewhere up the road, but it was too far away to tell what was going on. I thought no more of it and we all went home. The following morning, I learned that there had been an attack on a police officer with a hammer – a very serious incident.

I was asked to give evidence at the trial, despite having seen very little of what happened. All I could say was what I had seen – or not been able to see.

I was called to the Old Bailey where those accused of the attack were being tried. I duly took the stand and looked around. It was my first time in the Old Bailey and I found the courtroom to be quite intimidating, even for a witness. The prosecuting QC, James Crespi, questioned me and showed me photographs so I could identify where I had stood. For some reason, the police were claiming that the incident had happened where I was standing, rather than where it had in fact taken place – several hundred yards away, virtually out of sight. The defence barrister, Rudy Narayan, then questioned me, and the judge also asked a few questions in an avuncular tone. The four young men were acquitted.

I knew the police community liaison officer quite well and he told me that the outcome of the trial was a travesty of justice. I asked why the police had moved the crime scene to a different location, but he did not answer. I never found out the reason behind the police's insistence that the incident had happened some distance from where it had. I have no idea how much my evidence assisted the jury to come to its decision.

*

I received a fascinating insight into the health service when I was nominated to be a council member of the Kensington, Westminster and Chelsea Area Health Authority board. We had three teaching hospitals in our area and two or three mental health units. At that time, there was no concept of the role of chief executive, and the overall responsibility was shared among three people – the chief medical officer, chief finance officer and administrative officer. This was hardly a prescription for clear lines of accountability. Quite often, when questions were asked in meetings, the three looked at each other, unsure where the responsibility lay. I discovered that as members of the board, we were so far removed from day-to-day matters in the hospitals that our ability to have effective control was limited. On one occasion, I saw how medical politics really worked. We were trying to decide on the closure of a particular medical unit, couldn't agree and said we would have another meeting early one morning. When we arrived for the meeting, the deans of the three teaching hospitals told us they had met an hour previously, had agreed the key decision and left us with no choice but to agree with them.

But I discovered that it was sometimes possible to make positive changes in other areas. When the catchment area for our mental health hospital was being reviewed, I protested that a change of boundaries would mean the most disadvantaged people would be sent to a hospital in Surrey, miles from their families in Paddington, while the local facility would be available to those from middle-class areas. Everyone was taken aback by the vehemence of my argument but agreed with me. The social implications of tidying up a boundary had not been thought through. I was glad to be there as a councillor with a local mandate.

We uncovered what turned out to be one of the largest frauds against the health service up to that point. We appointed a communications manager at one of London's biggest hospitals, who had previously worked for the Queen. Perhaps that meant we did not vet him quite as thoroughly as we should have. In reviewing the financial figures at every meeting, we noticed that telephone expenditure was running far above budget. The communications manager reported he thought the problem was with cleaners who had easy access to the phones in the evening and were making long calls back to Jamaica. He assured us that this had been dealt with, but the figures kept showing above budgeted expenditure.

A more thorough investigation revealed that the communications manager had been diverting funds from the telephone budget to another account. He knew the system very well and had always arranged that the cheques would be presented at the last minute at the end of the month. He would personally approach the finance officers, saying that the cheque had to be cleared quickly, and could they overlook the fact that there wasn't a second signature on it. It was an astonishingly clever fraud, compounded by the fact that there appeared to be no safeguards against a cheque being diverted to a different bank account. We alerted the police, but by that time the person concerned had disappeared abroad, having defrauded the health authority of £100,000.

There was a further twist to this saga. He had installed a coffee and tea vending machine for the staff, but kept all the money that they had put into it to purchase their refreshments. The vending machine company said they were not receiving money, and they needed to be paid; again, he had made off with it. We established that he had no authority to arrange for the vending machine to be placed on the premises, so the health authority did not have to accept responsibility.

This abuse of the public purse was alarming, and it took an enormous amount of time to unravel, when we could have been doing more useful things for our local NHS hospitals. I was frustrated to see cash being spent on things other than helping patients. On another occasion, we wanted to dismiss the consultant of a mental health drop-in centre whose centre was failing its patients badly. Despite the overwhelming evidence against him, he was suspended on full pay for two years while the dismissal procedures ran their course.

I was part of Westminster City Council at a time when there much talk and disagreement as to what 'modernisation' of London should look like. There had been a fruit, vegetable and flower market at Covent Garden since the 1600s, but a plan to move it to a more accessible site in Nine Elms, south of the river, had been approved. The Covent Garden development scheme was created by the London County Council, which then became the Greater London Council.

In a move that sounds quire horrifying today, they intended to redevelop the site with a dual carriageway in place of Maiden Lane and a huge conference centre where the historic piazza sits. Fortunately, there was an outcry, and various groups came together to ensure the plans never went ahead. A good number of the old buildings in the area were added to the listed buildings register, which effectively stopped anyone trying to do something similar in the future. It's strange to think that without this activism, this historic and now upmarket area at the heart of central London was almost bulldozed.

There was another plan to reconfigure the layout of Piccadilly Circus, as the council was then obsessed with speeding up the traffic flow. A meeting was called in which the highly paid architects or planners showcased the proposed dual carriageway that would be built through the historic thoroughfare. I took an architect friend along with me, who was aghast. It was ridiculous to prioritise fast-flowing traffic right through the middle of London. Fortunately, this short-sighted idea met with enough resistance and commonsense prevailed. Otherwise, the West End would now be a very different place.

The battles over heritage ultimately reflect what we want our cities to look like, and are a reminder of the huge impacts – positive and negative – that councils can have. To some, planning permission might seem dull. But as a councillor, I saw how these decisions can have far-reaching effects on people's lives and into the future.

II.

There were two general elections in 1974, and I fought both of them as the candidate for South Hertfordshire.

It was a time of great turmoil in British politics. Ted Heath's Conservative government had decided to cap wages in the public sector to try to deal with very high levels of inflation. As the price of things continued to go up, this unsurprisingly proved unpopular, particularly with the miners. They went on strike in 1972, and once this had been concluded the unions banned overtime, which meant output went down, and Britain's coal-fired power stations started to run low on fuel. There was also an issue with oil imports due to embargoes following the Yom Kippur War, which had made Britain rather unpopular with the Arab oil-producing nations. In response, the government, taking a hard line against the unions, announced the three-day week would begin at the start of 1974 to conserve electricity. Businesses had to limit their energy use to three days within normal business hours. There were regular blackouts when we all had to sit by candlelight, keeping warm as best we could. It was not unlike wartime. Small businesses failed, there were lots of layoffs, and it was all pretty miserable.

Ted Heath called a snap election in the February with the aim of shoring up the government's power against the mineworkers' union. Labour set out in its campaign to convince the country that there was a way to build consensus and cooperation between the unions and the government. However, it didn't convince the country that much: Labour was voted in as a minority government, winning just four more seats that the Conservatives. Though not, unfortunately, in South Hertfordshire.

I ran against Cecil Parkinson, the sitting Conservative MP. The constituency was newly created just prior to this election, but the area had been Conservative for a long time. I was excited to be campaigning again, now with the experience of having fought one election under my belt, but it was not to be and I lost by 3,000 votes.

Then, in October, Harold Wilson called another general election. He had managed to bring the latest miners' strike to an end, but inflation was still very high and there was only so much that the government could get done without more MPs. I was once again the candidate for South Hertfordshire.

The outcome of the February election had made it clear that we should expect another to be called soon. So we were ready to go out again, knocking on doors, speaking to the same voters about the same issues. Fortunately, the South Hertfordshire Labour Party was very effective and energetic, ably chaired by Bryan Stanley, then general secretary of the Post Office Engineering Union. One Saturday morning, the much-loved jazz trumpeter Humphrey Lyttelton and his band led a march through Borehamwood High Street in support of the Labour Party. The shops emptied and people stood several feet deep to watch.

As election day approached, it still looked like a long shot that I could take the seat from Cecil Parkinson, but things felt closer than they had been back in February, and there was some optimism in the party. Some people from head office came down and seemed to think it was all going well. Though – privately, of course – I had my doubts.

Someone came up with the clever idea of delivering an eye-catching leaflet to registered Labour voters the day before the election that was designed to resemble a post office telegram – which were still just about in use in those days – to tell voters how close the polling was likely to be and hopefully inspire them to get out and vote. They were duly printed and delivered by local Labour Party members between 10 p.m. and 7 a.m. on 9–10 October. It is this support that gets one through the difficult times when campaigning, and I have been fortunate enough to make a lot of good friends in politics in this way over the years.

As I had thought, I did not win South Hertfordshire, even though I received more votes than I had in February's election.

Labour increased its share of seats in Parliament to become the majority party – by just three. A majority it would lose over the coming few years through various by-elections. Heath was eventually forced to resign as leader of the Conservative party, to be replaced by the MP for Finchley, Margaret Thatcher.

I went back to my work for the council and my job in Lewisham. I wondered if I would have another opportunity to run as an MP.

Towards the end of 1977 I learned that Battersea South was due to start the process of selecting a parliamentary candidate. The sitting MP, Ernie Perry, had decided to retire. Or perhaps 'decided' is a little strong – the local party had lost faith in him and he was eased out. I put my hat in the ring and was nominated by Earlsfield ward. But at the executive committee meeting, they crossed me off the list. My Earlsfield branch friends objected, saying I was the only candidate nominated by a ward that had not been shortlisted, so back on the list I went. I was regarded as a total outsider but in the event, I beat the local favourite, Mike Ward, by one vote. Mike was understandably very disappointed but quickly became supportive and remained a good friend, which says a great deal about his generosity of spirit.

When I became the prospective parliamentary candidate, Ernie Perry and Tom Cox, the MP for neighbouring Tooting, asked to meet me during party conference. It felt like an interrogation, and one of the things they wanted to know was where I stood on abortion. I told them I supported a woman's right to choose, and Ernie or Tom said, 'But you're not going to say that during the election, are you?' I responded that I could hardly deny my belief and that it wouldn't be a secret. They were from the Labour old guard and perhaps found it hard to understand that we were attracting new, younger members with different ideas and expectations.

Throughout 1978, the Labour government was finding it increasingly difficult to govern without a majority and while under mounting pressure from the unions. My friends in the Labour Party and I waited for news of when the election would be called, expecting it to happen that autumn. But though he was vulnerable, Callaghan held on. Then came the 'Winter of Discontent', with strikes leading to chaos. The image from that time many remember is rubbish piling up when refuse workers walked out. I sympathised with the unions, of course, but at the same time it was frustrating because it felt like the union leaders were doing everything possible to undermine the Labour government. The effect on public mood was such that voters would likely only go one way.

With an election imminent, as the new prospective candidate I thought we should make sure we were out canvassing. But the local party was understandably rather depressed; the Labour government was being pulled apart in the national press; there were even reports of bodies going unburied in Liverpool because the gravediggers were out on strike. I said I wouldn't go out canvassing alone, but we really had to do it. Gradually, more and more people pitched in and worked hard all the way through that terrible winter.

The Conservatives had been waiting for their opportunity, and on 28 March, the Labour government was defeated by a single vote in a no-confidence motion. Prime Minister James Callaghan went to the Queen to ask her to dissolve Parliament and the date for the general election was set for Thursday 3 May.

There had been mutterings that rather than retiring voluntarily, Ernie Perry had been the victim of a left-wing plot. That was a far too strong, but it was true that it wasn't entirely his decision to give up his seat. I tried to get on with him, and when the election was called, I asked if he would sign my nomination form. He paused for what seemed like a long time and then said, 'On one condition. That my name is first on the form.' To which I replied, 'That's the only place that I want your name.' During the campaign, the local press asked if it was true that Ernie had been ousted by a left-wing coup and that he wasn't supporting me, to which I was able to reply that his name was the first on my nomination form.

All the problems that the country was facing made for a difficult and yet very exciting campaign. Unemployment was thought to be shockingly high at 4.7 per cent (today it is around 5 per cent nationally), which led the advertising agency Saatchi and Saatchi to come up with the Conservative party's famous 'Labour Isn't Working' posters.

It's hard to describe what it was like campaigning at that

time. It was my fourth time campaigning for election, so I felt as confident as anyone ever can that I knew what I was doing. And this time I was fighting for a seat that was already held by Labour and, in theory, winnable. We realised that Battersea South had been targeted by the Tories, which galvanised more people to come and help to make sure we held it. As the newly selected candidate, it was my job to keep the local party energised, and I was very fired up to make the case for Labour to the electorate, but it was impossible to ignore the mood of the country. What's more, I was aware that this was probably my last opportunity. I was fairly sure that losing would mean I would not be selected again. I had overcome my previous doubts about putting myself forward as a candidate and won the nomination by a hair's breadth. But if I couldn't convince local voters, then it was over. And privately, I didn't like my chances. It was clear that there was going to be an overall swing to the Tories, and given that the 1974 majority was about 2,000, it felt like long odds that Labour would hold Battersea South.

My first job after selection had been to find an agent, as the previous one, Betty Malfoy, had decided to move on. The election agent is one of the few paid positions in campaigning. They organise meetings, look after the finances and decide where the canvassing should be targeted. It's a big role in a marginal seat. Fortunately, we found Ann Creighton, whose lack of experience was more than outweighed by her energy and enthusiasm.

During the campaign, I was delighted to see that we won the battle of the window bills – we had far more displayed than our opponents. Indeed, friends driving through south London during April that year told me that they knew they were in Battersea South by the 'Dubs. Labour' posters.

My wife Ann came out canvassing too, though we kept losing her as she would get involved in conversations with people. Ideally, you want to identify your supporters, make sure they intend to get out and vote, and move on as efficiently as possible, but without making anyone feel like you don't value them or are rushing off. Ann found it hard to extricate herself, and we'd often go back and find her embroiled in a long chat.

As the campaign went on, it became clear that neighbouring constituency Putney would probably go to the Conservatives, so disillusioned local activists started coming over to Battersea South to help with our campaign. They came from other parts of London too. While this didn't look good for the party overall, we did very much appreciate their help. We had committee rooms all over the place, with Ann Creighton and her helpers sending people out wherever they decided more volunteers were needed.

The weekend before an election is when things reach fever pitch. As a candidate, it is your responsibility to keep the energy levels high, no matter how exhausted you are. You must lead from the front, and if you flag, the campaign flags. There were about ten steps up to the party offices in Lavender

Hill, and I used to shoot up them two or three at a time. That would show everyone how keen and energised I was.

The Monday before the election is odd, though. You have made maximum effort over the weekend, always with a little voice in the back of your mind questioning whether you have done enough, and whether you are doing it right. Then you have three days until the polls open at 7 a.m. on the Thursday. You are completely exhausted but mustn't show it, and you have the prospect of staying up all night for the count looming ahead of you. The adrenaline is incredible.

But on Monday 30 April 1979, I was worried. The polls did not seem positive for the party overall. The ballots for Battersea North and Battersea South were counted in Battersea Town Hall. We had people out on the streets right up until the polls closed, trying to make sure everyone got out to vote – my election agent was very fierce on this point. But, as the candidate, there comes a point when all you can do is stand by the tables and watch, drinking as much coffee as you can bear.

We were glued to the radio as the results began to come in, and it didn't look good. I walked over to Douglas Jay, who was seeking re-election for Battersea North, and said, 'Douglas, I think I've had it.' He replied, 'Given the national swing, that is inevitable.' I thought, well, that's that. I won't be doing this again.

Feeling deflated and rather numb, I returned to the counting tables, where I noticed the counting had stopped. Then my agent rushed forward, shouting to our scrutineers from the local party looking over the count, 'Watch every ballot paper; there's going to be a recount!' She whispered to me, 'We're 300 up.'

News of the recount reached Wandsworth Town Hall, where votes for Wandsworth and Putney were being counted. The Tories there cheered, thinking that Labour had asked for the recount in Battersea South because we believed we were losing.

But actually, it was the Tories who were worried and who had asked for the recount. The ballots were recounted, and then the bundles were checked again. As I looked round the hall, the Tories seemed to be getting fewer and less cheerful. Soon, incredibly, it became apparent that Labour had won – albeit by only 332 votes after two recounts.

There were rumoured to have been six marginal Labour seats in London on the Conservative target list. They won five of these and others besides. However, for some reason, Battersea South stayed Labour. For a long time afterwards, people said it was the best constituency result for Labour in the entire election. And I owed that to Ann Creighton, the London regional organiser George Catchpole and a very loyal and energetic local party, as well as many Labour supporters who came to help from other constituencies.

Ann and I arrived home from the count, surprised and exhausted. Looking around, it dawned on us that what with the chaos of the past few days, we had no food in the house. So we thought we had better walk to the shops. While passing Porchester Hall, we bumped into friends from the Paddington Labour Party, who were leaving their count after a sixth recount. Arthur Latham had been the sitting MP for Paddington but had lost. It was strange to have won a narrow victory when so many were losing their seats. I felt sorry for Arthur, although I was aware that he was something of a casual attendee of local party meetings. He had a habit of giving a brief statement and taking a couple of questions before rushing off to the House for 'a vote' – though some of us knew there wasn't a vote that evening. I privately wondered whether he could have worked harder in his campaign and on his relationship with his local party members.

On the Saturday after the election, I did what my friend and council colleague Tim Daniel had taught me years before, after I was first elected as a councillor, and drove around the constituency with a loudspeaker. It was a lovely sunny day, so I stopped in various places to thank people for their support. I made the obvious point that although I was Labour, I was there to help everyone in the constituency. Of course, there is a reluctance to use loudspeakers nowadays because of their intrusive nature, and I didn't like doing it much, but for many years, long after any political statement I had made had been forgotten, people in Battersea would tell me that they remembered that I had driven round the constituency to thank them. When I stepped out of the car on the edge of Balham Market to thank people, I received a round of applause. It was lovely, if slightly embarrassing.

The only downside was that an egg was thrown at the car windscreen, I suspect by a National Front supporter. For anyone without experience of this, it is amazing how egg white turns opaque very quickly on a windscreen in the slight warmth of the sun. We had to spend a good twenty minutes cleaning it with newspaper so the car was safe to drive again. It was more amusing than frightening. I felt rather differently on polling day in 1983, when we were driving around the Patmore council estate, near Battersea Power Station, and a man working on a car threw a screwdriver at me. I was in the passenger seat with the window down, so he had a clear shot, but fortunately it missed and hit the side of the old taxi we were using as our campaign vehicle. The force of it left a dent in the bodywork, which was better than in my face, at which it was aimed.

I hadn't expected to win the seat. And so I hadn't allowed myself to think that far ahead or really consider the implications of becoming an MP. My first task was to return to Lewisham to resign from my job and clear my desk. My boss there had been incredibly supportive and had offered me as much time off as I needed for the campaign.

I broached the idea of moving my family to Battersea, as I was keen to live in the constituency. But they quite reasonably argued that they didn't want to have to move house and go to new schools just so I could get home twenty minutes earlier in the evening. So we stayed in Paddington, which was only about three miles north of Battersea anyway. I took pride in never going ex-directory during my time as an MP, but I told my children to be careful of phone calls.

In truth, I felt rather unprepared to enter the House of Commons as a member of the British Parliament. The prospect of learning how the business of the House was conducted and what was expected of one as an MP was daunting. As I recovered from the hard work of the campaign and 'came down' from the excitement of winning my seat for the party, I anticipated a steep learning curve ahead.

III.

As a new MP, one faces the obvious initial challenges of finding one's way around, discovering where one is expected to be and when, and trying to get a sense of who will be helpful and who less friendly. It is somewhat comparable with starting at a new school. So perhaps it was useful that I had done that many times.

Parliament is an amazing building, and I was excited to be entering as an elected representative. I still love working within it. But it is important not to be too overawed, or self-congratulatory, and to remember that the only purpose of being there is to change things for the better. In order to be effective, I would need to quickly learn how the House of Commons functioned.

Feeling smug was perhaps less of a danger for my intake of new Labour MPs. There was a pervading sense of gloom as we went into opposition. It was an odd feeling to have succeeded in winning my seat when others I knew had been defeated. And even if one is feeling rather pleased with oneself, there will always be a moment to puncture any self-importance, as I soon learned one evening a few weeks after the election when I arrived for an all-night debate. As I reached the entrance to the Commons, a police officer said, 'Good evening, Sir.' To which I replied, 'Good evening,' adding with all the pomposity of a newly elected MP, 'I am hoping to speak tonight.' 'Yes, sir,' she said. 'Will it make any difference?' Duly humbled, I went into the chamber. At nearly 6 a.m., I made my speech about the inner city, jobs, housing and cuts to local government. It made not the slightest difference.

My first task was to deal with the logistics of setting up an office. First, I had to find one. Space was very limited, and I spent the first weeks carrying around all my things, with nowhere to put anything. Our allowances were sufficient for only a half-time secretary, and mine was very overworked. It took me a few days to find the Post Office in the Commons. When I did, they presented me with a mountain of letters that had arrived immediately after the election. I quickly realised that the tearoom is an important institution where one could learn the ropes. You could meet colleagues over cups of tea to exchange political gossip. In those days, the ex-miners all sat together.

Jim Callaghan had wanted to resign after the election defeat but was persuaded to stay on to ease the transition to the next leader. Callaghan asked to see the newly elected

MPs individually. We had a long and friendly chat. He asked me what I was interested in, to which I replied 'inner-city issues', given the nature of my constituency. He asked if I might consider widening my interests and include a topic like afforestation. I questioned this, perhaps not very politely, as there was no constituency basis for that kind of interest. Looking back, I realise that Jim was much wiser than I had thought. He said at the time that he had no one in the PLP (Parliamentary Labour Party) who he could turn to on that issue. In the years since, it has become crucially important in terms of climate change and flooding. I sometimes wish I had acted on his advice.

I found myself frequently sitting next to him in the Commons after he had stood down as leader and thought he was an incredibly wise politician. I asked him why he had not called the election in the autumn of 1978 rather than the spring of 1979, as had been expected. His answer was that all the evidence suggested that he would have lost in 1978, so why should a prime minister call an election that he expected to lose? There was no answer to that, and nobody could have expected the winter of 1978–9 to have been so damaging to the Labour Party.

On another occasion, I had a question put down to the prime minister, which was high up on the list to be called at PMQs (Prime Minister's Questions). Jim suggested that he would then ask a follow-up question, known as a 'supplementary', to support me. I asked why rates of crime had gone up every year under Thatcher, while they had gone down under Callaghan? Thatcher was caught out on statistics, even though she was a scientist. It was one of the rare times I saw her on the back foot, unsure how to respond. Jim then came in with a further supplementary which pushed her into a corner. Some of my colleagues praised me for this, but it was entirely down to Jim's political acumen.

Thinking back on that time, I feel bad that I did not sufficiently appreciate Jim's many excellent qualities. He took over the leadership of the Labour Party at a difficult time; I am sure that if circumstances were otherwise, he would have been a successful prime minister for many years.

While most legislation originates with the government, there are also opportunities for back-benchers. There are various ways of introducing legislation as a private member's bill. After each King's Speech, there is a ballot that MPs can enter, but only the top half-dozen or so have any chance of securing time for a debate and progressing towards becoming law. An example is the Terminally Ill Adults [End of Life] Bill, which passed through all its stages in the Commons, but was blocked by procedural tactics in the Lords in 2026. Another method is the Ten-Minute Rule Bill. This gives an MP a chance at peak time in the afternoon to make a short speech introducing a private member's bill. This almost never becomes law, but it is a good way to draw attention to an issue and possibly influence government thinking.

In those days, it was possible to get a slot that enabled

one to speak just after Questions in the afternoon – so long as you were the first person in the Public Bill Office at 10 a.m. This was often a matter of luck. I once arrived at 9.55 a.m. to find nobody there, but on another occasion, I arrived at 11.30 p.m. when the House had risen, intending to spend the night at the head of the queue, to find I had been beaten to it by another MP.

I was still inexperienced when on 20 November I introduced a bill to explicitly ban jury vetting. This was a practice whereby officials would look at lists of potential jurors and delete those who appeared to be 'unfavourable to a successful prosecution' – based on things like their ethnicity, the neighbourhood of their registered address or their gender. It was, to my mind, borderline corruption. The prosecution were effectively stacking the jury with those they felt were more likely to decide in their favour, something which is completely against the fundamental principle of someone being tried by twelve of their peers selected at random. I had first learned about it through a constituent who had complained about the practice. The government eventually claimed that the practice had been stamped out, but then I received a letter from a prisoner in jail saying that his jury had been vetted prior to his conviction. I raised the matter again in the House and the Attorney General, Michael Havers MP, admitted that there had been a slip-up and that he would ensure that it would never happen again.

One of the most satisfying things that I did during those

early years in the Commons was serving on the Home Affairs select committee. Shortly after the 1979 election, Norman St John-Stevas, the Leader of the House, introduced a significant change – the establishment of departmental select committees, cross-party groups of back-benchers that would scrutinise the work of the department they were attached to. I heard, though cannot confirm, that they were brought in somewhat under the leadership's radar and that Margaret Thatcher did not realise what was happening until the new committees were in place. Apparently she was very annoyed about the prospect of government ministers being subject to additional and tougher scrutiny.

The Home Affairs committee covered things like policing, prisons and immigration – very much my areas of interest. I had tried to get onto the committee soon after arriving in Parliament but I wasn't immediately successful. Other candidates who had been somewhat surer of winning their seats had been doing things like taking meetings with the whips in the run-up to the election; I was rather more concerned with the campaign itself and trying to do my day job at Lewisham council, and rather less certain of my chances of becoming an MP at all. But then there was a vacancy, and I managed to get myself selected.

I was on the committee for a number of years and found it a politically satisfying experience. At Question Time in the Commons, I might ordinarily get the chance to ask the Home Secretary something once every few months, whereas as part of the select committee, I sometimes could interrogate the Home Secretary for five minutes or so on a particular issue. Nowadays, I always advise people in either House they should get onto a select committee if they can, because I think it's a marvellous opportunity to learn and to get to the heart of important issues.

Standing committees (now called public bill committees) are different to select committees in that they only exist to deal with the committee stage of a particular bill and, if necessary, to amend the bill. In 1981, I was selected by the whips to serve on the British Nationality Bill standing committee. There was a need to reform the whole issue of British citizenship, as the existing situation was confusing and outdated – very much influenced by the legacy of the British Empire. It was not without its controversies, but the question of who was entitled to British subject status was nowhere near as fraught or emotionally charged as the debates we see now about British citizenship. I am now on the House of Lords Justice and Home Affairs Committee, and so still looking at British citizenship and identity.

At the time, I could not help reflecting on the irony that here was a naturalised Brit serving on the committee that would determine the future of British citizenship. What other country would have made this possible? My mother had become naturalised sometime in the late 1940s, as many displaced people were in the aftermath of the war, and, as a minor and a dependent, I was automatically included in that.

Then, when I came of age the Home Office sent me a piece of paper which asked if I wanted to give up or retain my British citizenship. At the bottom was a little tear-off slip that said, 'I do / do not wish to renounce my British citizenship'. You just ticked a box on a tiny slip and sent it back. So I sent it off, and that was it. I was British.

On one occasion, members of the Home Affairs select committee were sent to Chicago to study both the ethnic question in the population census and the racial composition of the Chicago police. At that time, there was opposition to having a question on ethnicity in the British Population Census. The concept of 'ethnicity' is always going to be a somewhat complex one and open to interpretation. That is unavoidable. Some at the time felt that asking people was wrong, as it could increase the chances of prejudice, or just that it was none of the government's business. Some even thought that, should the National Front come to power, it could be a problem for those in ethnic minorities to be easily identifiable in the census. My feeling was that you can't do much good unless you have the data available to show you where the need or inequality is. A good example of this was a survey of council housing done around this time which demonstrated that black people had a lesser chance of getting council housing, or if they got it, it was of inferior quality. The evidence of such blatant discrimination strengthened the case for an ethnic question on the population census.

In Chicago, we saw this in action, and we learned that the

black community believed that the census was the best strategy they had. We were given two examples of when this data had proved vital.

The first concerned the proposed re-warding of parts of Chicago. The census information had revealed that cynical gerrymandering was behind the proposed boundaries, as they would create two wards with a white majority and one with a black one.

The second example concerned the aftermath of a very cold spell, which brought commuter trains to a halt. When they were restarted, the transport people decided that to speed things up, the trains from the more distant commuter belt would not stop in the inner suburbs on the way downtown. Thanks to census data, it was easy to see that the trains would bring white commuters into work but bypass the black community, who had an equal need, and the practice was quickly altered. Again, the data provided by the census was essential for exposing inequality and making the right decisions. We came back fully convinced of the merits of an ethnicity question in the census and provided the arguments that later led to its introduction.

Through our meetings with the Chicago police, we learned how they ensured an annual recruitment of black and other minority ethnic people into the police force. We also gained a real insight into gangs and criminality.

Although it was fascinating to observe policing in Chicago, there were other incidents that did not reflect so well on the less specialised police officers. We were walking in daylight and saw a black man drinking something like vodka out of a bottle. A police officer snatched the bottle from him, poured it onto the pavement, muttered something about it being an inferior brand and said sarcastically, 'You are a fine example of your race.'

While in the Commons, I became particularly interested in penal reform and joined the All-Party Parliamentary Group on Penal Affairs, becoming its vice chair. At that time, the prison population was growing and we became increasingly concerned when the figure reached 44,000, which was then a very high figure – today it is 87,000. I once went to Wormwood Scrubs and entered a cell where three young men were lying on their bunks for twenty-three hours every day. The sense of hopelessness about their situation, without work or anything else for them to do, was powerful.

In contrast, I visited the Barlinnie Special Unit in Glasgow. It was famous for its work in rehabilitation and the relationships between prisoners and prison officers, which were relaxed and on first-name terms. The head of the special unit showed me a large mural on the wall depicting workers in factories producing goods, making a profit for their owners, who invested in more factories to produce more goods, and so on. In other words, capitalism. The head of the unit said to me half-jokingly, 'They come in here as villains and leave as socialists.'

While the Barlinnie Special Unit showed what the penal system was capable of, unfortunately, the unit was eventually closed because it was deemed to be too expensive. I suspect a more rigorous analysis might have demonstrated that, in terms of benefits to the overall community and lower rates of recidivism, it probably represented quite good value.

The early years of the 1980s remained a febrile time in British politics. When Margaret Thatcher's government was first elected, there was no sense of how far to the right she would take her party. The concept of 'Thatcherism' and all it would entail for the unions, the miners and so many in society had not yet crystallised. At the beginning of the decade, opinion polls showed her government was highly unpopular.

In the Labour Party, there was a growing gulf between the hard left and the centrists. I, and many others, felt that there was an urgent need to unite the party if we were to defeat the government in the next election. In 1980, Denis Healey had lost the leadership contest to Michael Foot, as it was thought that Michael would have a better chance of appealing to a broader cross-section of the party, whereas Denis's style was more confrontational.

I voted for Michael. He was a wonderful human being, a brilliant writer and a passionate socialist, but he lacked important qualities of leadership and did not heal the rifts in the party as we had hoped. The Tories vilified him. At an Armistice Day commemoration at the Cenotaph in Whitehall, Michael wore what looked like a duffle coat, in contrast to other party leaders who wore more formal overcoats.

The Tories and the conservative press poured scorn on Michael, saying it was disrespectful to wear a donkey jacket on such a solemn occasion.

The SDP (Social Democratic Party) was formed in 1981, during my first term in the Commons. It was led by the 'Gang of Four' – Roy Jenkins, David Owen, Bill Rodgers and Shirley Williams –- and was set up to damage, if not destroy, the Labour Party. Every week or so, the Gang of Four persuaded a couple of Labour MPs to defect. It was a most miserable time for us all, and our nerves were on edge as we waited to see who the next defector would be. I was approached to join, and replied very angrily that I had just been elected as a Labour MP and was not going to betray the people who had voted for me or my principles. It still feels wrong that an MP representing their party and voted in by their constituents should jump ship in the middle of a parliamentary term.

The Argentinians invaded the Falkland Islands on 2 April 1982. It was a moment of high drama, although we had no sense then of the repercussions the conflict would have on British politics. Parliament was recalled for a Saturday sitting. With hardly any exceptions, everyone was in the mood for military action. As the Task Force was assembled and set off for the South Atlantic, there was jingoism in the air. I found the situation agonising. A small group of us met in the Commons because we wanted more time for negotiations. As we sat and discussed our tactics, journalists sent by the popular papers were stationed outside the committee rooms, taking note of who was in attendance. *The Sun* printed photographs of our small group with snide comments underneath, such as 'Best known for being coy about her age'. I got away with: 'Thinks he champions human rights'.

War heightens everyone's emotions. There was consternation when an MP accused us of being guilty of treason because we did not come out in full support of the war. The group started talking about raising money for legal action. I demurred. To my mind, being accused of treason was a political comment, nothing more than rather hysterical grandstanding. If I had been accused of shoplifting, I said, it could have been much more damaging, as it might have been believed. Nonetheless, the others said they would sue. Later in the day, however, Tony Benn came up to me and said that on reflection, he agreed with me. The legal action never happened.

We agreed that as the Task Force approached the South Atlantic, we would consider voting against the government's motion for military action. I agreed to vote on the basis that we wanted more time for negotiations, but would not do so after British troops were involved in action because it would undermine them. In the meantime, there was turmoil in the wider Labour Party. The Battersea General Committee was divided on the issue. It was a close call, but in the end, partly out of loyalty, it backed my position. Some letters of support arrived, but I did also receive a white feather in the post.

Then Tyne Tees television invited me to take part in their Friday evening current affairs programme *Friday Night Live*.

As I left my constituency surgery to get to Newcastle, I had no idea what awaited me. The format of the programme was a panel of eight, audience participation and phone-in votes. Of the panel, six were for military action, and my sole colleague in opposition was a brother of a Tory minister and an apologist for General Galtieri, the Argentinian dictator. What I had not been warned about was that many of the audience had sons in the convoy out in the South Atlantic. I was accused of being a coward. I protested that I was not being asked to fight, but that their sons were brave men who shouldn't be pushed into fighting if a peaceful solution was available. Only two people in the audience supported me – one a trade unionist, the other a vicar who was the local CND chair. The voting was heavily weighted against my view when the programme started. By the time it finished, I had persuaded nobody, and there were even more people against my position. It was a bruising experience which taught me that when emotions are running high, having a rational debate becomes very difficult.

After the programme, I returned to my hotel in Newcastle and received a message from David Clark, a parliamentary colleague. He had seen me on the programme, tracked me down and invited me to walk along the Roman Wall with him the following day. He didn't necessarily agree with my position, but such companionship was welcome, and the walk calmed me down. I don't regret the stance I took, although I must concede that losing the war enabled Argentina to oust Galtieri, a particularly nasty dictator.

After the Argentinians had been defeated, I was invited to join a parliamentary delegation to the Falkland Islands. At that time, it involved a twenty-seven-hour flight with in-air refuelling. When Michael Cocks MP, the Labour Chief Whip, asked me about my health and whether I could stand such a long flight, I said yes. I then told him that I was particularly keen to go as I had voted against the government. His reaction was immediate – he vetoed my attendance. John Gilbert MP had organised the visit, and although he supported the government line on this, he did say that it was a pity that an opponent of the position could not be a member of the delegation.

When the Task Force returned to Britain and the SS *Canberra* sailed up Southampton Water, there were enormous celebrations, with much public support for the Thatcher government. The sense that Britain had something to be proud of again turned the tide. Had Margaret Thatcher not recaptured the Falklands, I firmly believe that she would not have been re-elected as prime minister.

Despite the public mood, following the general election in June 1983 I increased my majority in Battersea to around 3,000. Boundary changes had meant the merging of Battersea North and South, with some of the southern wards going into Tooting. But though we had been ahead in the polls prior to the war in the Falklands, the party suffered a landslide defeat. The Tories had placed Margaret Thatcher front and centre of the campaign, with her new 'Iron Lady' persona on full display. Michael Foot's more casual style was in direct contrast. On the left, the alliance of the SDP and the Liberals had siphoned off votes that might have gone to Labour.

Morale in the Labour Party was even lower than in 1979, and the divisions continued. I, along with many others, felt that we had an urgent job to heal the problems within the party and needed to have much more sensible conversations. On the far left, the Militant group, a faction within the Party, had taken control of Liverpool City Council and now had two MPs in Parliament.

Avowed Marxists, they were said to be inspired by Trotsky, the revolutionary who met a sticky end when Stalin had him murdered with an ice pick in Mexico. There was a big row about how it was acting as a party-within-a-party and threatening to take over the agenda.

Then there was Tony Benn, sometimes brilliant but at other times he espoused some left-wing causes without compromise. There were very few Militants in the Battersea Party, but over the borough boundary in Lambeth the situation was different, and it had a knock-on effect in our area. One extreme left-winger turned up as a member of the Labour Party in the Balham branch. When I said that I had not voted for Tony Benn to enter the Shadow Cabinet, he jumped on the platform, denounced me and said I should immediately be deselected. Subsequently, news about demands for my deselection appeared in the local press. At the next General Committee meeting, I said that we should resolve our differences within the party and not use the capitalist press to attack one another. Silence. One person said, 'We can't touch you now, Alf, can we?'

Neil Kinnock needed an office from which to run his campaign for leadership. Space was at a premium in those days, so Frank Dobson, with whom I shared an office, suggested they put another desk in ours. I liked Neil a lot and believed he could bring us all back together. After he won the leadership, I was appointed to his Home Affairs front-bench team.

In October 1985, he made his famous speech at the Bournemouth conference in which he attacked Militant-controlled Liverpool City Council. The council had started a huge project of house building and hired many workers, refusing the budget cuts imposed on it by central government. But it went too far, using the threat of redundancies as a bargaining chip against the government, which backfired. Neil was furious and demanded unity across the party. We needed a focus on re-election above all else, he argued; it was the only way to help people suffering amid Tory cuts. He denounced the actions of the Liverpool Militants, saying, 'You end up in the grotesque chaos of a Labour council – a *Labour* council – hiring taxis to scuttle round a city handing out redundancy notices to its own workers.' I was sitting behind Neil when he delivered this marvellous speech and saw the reaction. There was enormous applause, but some boos and jeers from the Militants. NEC Member and Liverpool Walton MP Eric Heffer stormed off the platform.

In a conference vote, the Militants were defeated by 6 million to half a million votes. My good friend Frank Dobson MP approached Hatton and Mulhearn, the two leading Militants, and asked them what they thought about the vote. They didn't answer, so Frank interjected, 'Six million ice picks can't be wrong.'

I'd already had something of a run-in with Eric Heffer by this point. On 29 May 1985, a wall in Heysel Stadium in Brussels collapsed before the kick-off of the European Cup final, in which Liverpool FC were playing Juventus. Ninety-seven people died, and hundreds were injured. As a member of the opposition front-bench team I was asked to deal with the media in the immediate aftermath. I did several interviews in which I said it was a terrible tragedy and there had to be a full inquiry to establish the facts and to see how such a thing could be prevented from happening again. Later that day, I ran into Eric Heffer, who asked me what I thought I was doing without consulting him first, as the MP for Liverpool and Walton. I pointed out that we had to be quick at responding to media requests and it wouldn't have been possible to check everything with him first. He said, 'They are all my people. They are working class from Liverpool.' I replied, 'Yes. And I was measured in my comments. And I thought the Juventus football fans were also working class.' Eric astonished me by saying, 'What do you know about it?'

And then he stormed off.

*

Arthur Scargill had taken over as General Secretary of the National Union of Mineworkers (NUM) in April 1982, and the mood was increasingly confrontational. Margaret Thatcher was determined to get her own back for the miners' previous victories over governments, including that of her predecessor, Ted Heath. Scargill knew that the strikes of 1974 had brought down the Heath government and was clearly in the mood to do the same to the Tories in 1984. He was determined to lead a strike against the pit closures announced by the Conservative government, but not all the regions were in favour. So instead of holding a decisive national ballot of the NUM, which he feared he would lose, he prompted a series of local ones.

When the strike was called, it was hard to believe it. It began in March, the time of the year when the seasonal demand for coal was falling, so the unions had less industrial muscle. Other unions declined to take sympathetic strike action because not all the miners had stopped work. The Nottinghamshire pits stayed open, so the NUM picketed the Nottinghamshire miners, without success. Scenes of miners picketing miners only added to a sense of chaos and disunity.

In 1984, I was invited to visit Nicaragua ahead of the elections that November. I was to be one of a small team of international observers. President Reagan had supported the Contras in what was effectively a civil war against the leftist Sandinista government, even though they had managed to get rid of the evil Somoza regime.

We visited different parts of the country in the build-up

to the elections. In Managua, I attended a large Sandinista election rally with their leader, Daniel Ortega. I was on a platform behind him, and it was an exciting occasion. I met Thomas Borge, the Interior Minister, whose office walls were covered with crucifixes of different designs. I could not decide whether this was because of his religious beliefs or just to give the impression that he held them. I also met Nora Astorga, who had been an important guerrilla fighter and was linked to the murder of a notorious womanising senior officer in Somoza's National Guard. She later became the Sandinista government's ambassador to the UN.

On polling day, 4 November 1984, we observed the closing of the polls and the count. Understandably, the staff at the polling stations were nervous of foreign observers, especially as it was the first time they had handled an election. It was an emotional ceremony as everyone sang the national anthem before opening the ballot boxes. Then there was consternation when the total number of votes in one of the ballot boxes was one short of the number of ballot papers issued. The tellers were distraught, so I tried to reassure them, through an interpreter, that such discrepancies were common in Britain, and did not necessarily undermine the integrity of the poll.

The Sandinistas had a great victory and started a major literacy campaign, as well as improving health services and land reform. However, in later years, some of their leaders, including Daniel Ortega, seemed to lose their revolutionary fervour, adopting reactionary policies regarding the rights of women, particularly on abortion, and suppressing civil rights. The government is now widely condemned by human rights organisations as an authoritarian regime.

I brought back some unused ballot papers from Nicaragua; I think they had been printed in Sweden, and were beautiful works of art. I found that auctioning them at Labour Party and trade union meetings was an easy way of fundraising for the miners' union, and encouraged solidarity between Nicaragua and the miners.

From early in the strike, Battersea Labour Party was twinned with Whitwell, a north Derbyshire colliery in Dennis Skinner's constituency of Bolsover. On one occasion, we were invited up to Whitwell to show our support. I went up with Labour Party colleagues and a car boot full of food. As we drove north, we passed columns of coaches bringing police officers back to London from the coalfields. The government had said over and over that we did not have national policing in Britain, that every force was responsible for its own community. However, it was clear that the Home Office had arranged with ACPO (the Association of Chief Police Officers) beforehand to coordinate police activity across the country. There was something quite ominous about the way in which the police had been mobilised to control the picket lines.

We helped at the Miners' Welfare Centre and went to the Butcher's Arms pub in the centre of the village, where I said a few words supporting the miners and complimenting the people on Dennis Skinner, their local MP. I said something about wanting to emulate him, to which one of the older miners commented, 'It'll take thee a long time, lad.' I then went to my host's home. He was a militant miner, and was on curfew for an offence connected with picketing, so had to be back by 10 p.m. We talked long into the night over bacon sandwiches. We discussed the strike and I asked about the ballot, or lack of one. The miner replied, 'There's lots of us here think that there should have been a ballot, but we can't say so in present circumstances.' Early in the morning, we were on the picket line at Whitwell Colliery. The strike was virtually complete, save for half a dozen scabs.

In the late summer of 1984, I was at a small conference at Balliol College, Oxford, where I spoke to David Howell, who had been Energy Secretary for two years at the start of Margaret Thatcher's first term in office. He told me that the current Energy Secretary, Peter Walker, had told the Tory MPs that provided it wasn't the coldest winter in history and that the transport unions were willing to move imported coal, the government could hold out indefinitely. Did Scargill know this? I asked. David said he must have done so, as he had access to the same information the government had regarding the coal stockpiles.

At one point, there was a possibility of a deal offered by the government that would have given the miners at least something. But Scargill turned it down. For the miners, the inevitable catastrophe occurred and they were forced back to work, with disastrous consequences. While many of us supported the miners, we recognised that Scargill's policies proved devastating for his members and their families.

Politics effectively stopped in Britain for a year because of the miners' strike. Opinions differed and still do as to whether a national ballot early on would have won the day, and whether there might then have been sympathetic action from other unions. Above all, I believe the miners deserved better than to be caught in a battle between Margaret Thatcher and Arthur Scargill. She had wanted to close an entire industry regardless of the consequences, and in the process, thought she could seriously weaken the unions. He thought he could bring down the government. No one was pushing for a better deal for pit villages or working on a plan to ensure economic security. It was inevitable that British mines would come under pressure from cheaper imports and other energy sources – mainly gas, plus some nuclear at this point. The result was that thousands of miners' livelihoods disappeared and their villages became virtual wastelands. Years after the pits had closed, I drove through Whitwell village, which I had visited in 1984, and felt a general sadness about the place.

IV.

Battersea had long been an industrial area, but during the 1960s and 70s, many of the large factories closed down, and manufacturing moved out of London. Battersea South, where I won my seat in 1979, was a mixed bag compared to the more solidly working-class Battersea North. Whereas the area along the Thames, once lined with large factories, was the scene of visible industrial decline from about the 1970s, around Clapham and Wandsworth commons there was more solid Victorian housing stock. It began to attract middle-class homebuyers, starting a process of gentrification.

In my first term as an MP, my colleague in the North Battersea seat was Douglas Jay, who was first elected in 1946. Some twenty-five years my senior, Douglas had been to Winchester and Oxford, and joined the Labour Party in the early 1930s. His politics and mine were somewhat different but I maintained enormous respect for him. Some General

Committee members tried, mischievously, to pit us against one another, but I did my best to prevent any obvious rows between us. For his part, he was unfailingly helpful and supportive of me throughout the 1979–83 Parliament.

Douglas had some engaging eccentricities, one of which was that he always wore incredibly scruffy suits that looked like they had been rejected by Oxfam. In fact, he was a serious and highly intelligent politician.

On one occasion, I saw that some Irish Republicans had put up a banner on the railings opposite the party offices. Two protestors from their midst came into my surgery and took their turn among people with housing problems, difficulties with social security and immigration. When I established that they lived in Battersea North, they said they would come back the following Friday to see Douglas. I later heard that it resulted in quite an acrimonious meeting, especially as Douglas had little sympathy for the Irish cause.

Douglas retired in 1983, when the boundary changes merged Battersea North and South. Ahead of the 1983 general election, Matthew Parris, a Tory MP who happened to live in my constituency, wrote to me and warned me that because of the increased 'yuppification' of the constituency, I was in danger of losing my seat. It was a kind and helpful letter, more so as it came from a Conservative politician. In the end, I won comfortably, but while my majority of 3,000 votes looked good on paper, in reality, given the inclusion of the council estates near the river, it should have been much more. It was a sign not just of the increased popularity of Margaret Thatcher after the Falklands War, but of how the area was changing.

Housing was one of the most pressing issues in my constituency, as it still is in many areas of London. The 1980 Housing Act had given tenants the right to buy their home from the local council, which allowed some to get on what we would learn to call 'the property ladder'. Though, of course, for many, this still remained out of reach. Meanwhile, central government restricted the amount of money local authorities could borrow, which limited their ability to build new housing stock. Encouraged by Conservative doctrine, private developers stepped into the gap.

In 1978, the outgoing Labour council had wanted the site of the huge recently closed Morgan Crucible plant, which one could see when crossing from Chelsea to Battersea on Battersea Bridge, to be designated for public housing. There was quite a row about this. Peter Shore, then Labour's Secretary of State for the Environment, gave permission for houses to be built on the site, but there were no safeguards in place to prevent a private developer from acquiring it. By the time I became the MP, unfortunately, it was slated for luxury housing.

On the Battersea Bridge Road edge of the site, there was a long wall on which Brian Barnes, a local artist, had painted a mural, with the help of people from the local community. It was a wonderful depiction of workers fighting for their rights with a resounding socialist message. A local campaign to save it from the developer and position it elsewhere was started. During a demo against the wall's demolition, Councillor Christopher Chope, then leader of the Tory council, came to have a look. He was quickly chased away by angry demonstrators. One police officer confessed that the police had no idea that there would be such an outcry about the wall's proposed demolition. I could have warned them.

About three weeks after the 1979 election, bulldozers were sent in to demolish the wall. I had been clearing up the election accounts with my agent, Ann, when we heard what was happening and rushed to the scene. By the time we arrived half the wall had gone, and Brian Barnes was standing on top of the remainder, defying the bulldozers. The police had closed off Battersea Bridge and the immediate area as if it were a terrorist incident, and crowds began to gather. We never forgave the developer, nor the Tory Council. The mural could have been saved and moved elsewhere. It seemed symbolic of what was to befall the area as 'progress' marched swiftly on, as more and more expensive housing was built for those who could afford it.

The pattern continued. Behind Clapham Junction there was a council estate, the Livingstone estate. Asbestos was discovered in it, and quite properly, the residents, who were mostly Afro-Caribbean, were moved out. However, they were never allowed to move back in. When the asbestos had been removed, the block was sold to a private developer, Regalian Properties, who renamed it 'The Falcons' and made it into a gated development for affluent people. The Tory council gave a big party to celebrate the new development. However, people on the council's waiting list had to wait much longer for housing because the available stock had been reduced. Dai Goldstone, the head of Regalian Properties, had been an undergraduate with me at the LSE and had always claimed to be a left-wing socialist from South Wales. Of course, very few Labour voters were to be found in the exclusive development his company created. I pointed out to him that he was helping me to lose my seat.

A very visible symbol of the changing fortunes of Battersea is, of course, the iconic power station, a building that has characterised Battersea since the first stage was completed in 1935, and whose journey exemplifies the economic and political changes of the last four decades. It was made a Grade II listed building by Michael Heseltine in 1980 when he was Secretary of State for the Environment. The Central Electricity Generating Board stopped using it in 1983 and decided to dispose of the building. The plan was to have a competition for its future use, and the people behind the winning entry would acquire the building for a song. I wrote to the CEGB urging them to include a reversion clause in the contract so that if the winning consortium could not proceed with their development, the building would revert to the public sector. It was listed, and estimated at the time to be on a valuable green field site. The CEGB replied that the reversion clause would not be necessary as planning controls would be a sufficient safeguard.

The winning consortium very quickly failed to deliver, and the building was sold on to another developer, the owner of Alton Towers, for £1.5 million in 1987. This developer removed the roof, leaving the building exposed to the elements. Our suspicion was that this had been done deliberately; if the building could be deemed a dangerous structure, it could be pulled down. There would then be a vast capital gain through having an empty site to develop, with no iconic power station to work around. Margaret Thatcher said that the new developer exemplified the best of British business and that she would attend the opening ceremony even if it was several years away. I still have a poster calling us to demonstrate at the gates of Thatcher's alleged opening ceremony. But beyond the removal of the roof, nothing happened.

Six years later, Parkview, a Hong Kong-based company bought the site and invited me to their Mayfair offices to see models of what they proposed. The company assured me that by the autumn they would be able to raise the money to proceed with their development. Unsurprisingly, again nothing happened, and the site was then bought by an Irish company. With each sale, an increasing sum of money changed hands. Profit was going into the pocket of each successive owner, but the building remained empty and the site was not developed. The Irish company could not raise the money because of the financial crisis, and eventually, a Malaysian company bought the site, again for an increased sum. In the meantime, I consulted English Heritage about the need to safeguard the power station as a listed building. They assured me that everything would be all right.

Over the years, I initiated debates in the Commons and the Lords on the issue. A local group was established, the Battersea Power Station Community Group, which campaigned very actively on behalf of the community. We were concerned that any resulting development should provide maximum employment opportunities to the local community and a stake in its benefits.

Work finally began sometime around 2013, thirty years after the power station closed. But in the end, most of the residential accommodation around the site is expensive. Little affordable housing was planned to be constructed on the site, and social housing was not due to be built until the third stage of development. The luxury apartments attracted speculators; one news item reported that a studio flat had been sold off-plan for £1 million and six months later was resold, still off-plan, for £1.5 million. In 2022 the commercial parts of the redevelopment finally began to open. Margaret Thatcher was not able to attend; she had died nine years earlier.

My own preference for the power station was to develop it as an arts centre, with additional galleries for the National Gallery and possibly the V&A, and a mix of housing, including affordable homes. In fact, given that Transport for London extended the underground to the area, it could even have rivalled the very successful development achieved for Tate Modern. In the meantime, the Nine Elms Lane area has come up in the world, and the US Embassy is now situated there.

*

I held four constituency surgeries a month in different locations around Battersea. They were always drop-ins, and people came without appointment. In some constituencies, people will first approach the council and then seek out the assistance of their MP to resolve their issue if that fails, and in others, such as Battersea, there was more of a tradition of going straight to your MP.

In the mid-1980s, Sainsbury's was concentrating on developing large out-of-town superstores and closing smaller ones. There was a medium-sized store in Balham that was at risk of closure, and the Battersea Labour Party ran a petition asking Sainsbury's to keep it open. Many people could not shop by car, and the small store served the local community very well. As a result, Sainsbury's agreed the store could continue trading for a trial period of six months. This proved such a success that it stayed open. It is still there and has been redeveloped over the years, no doubt to the supermarket chain's great advantage. Unfortunately, my suggestion that the Battersea Labour Party receive a share of the increased profits that Sainsbury's had made because of our intervention was not taken up.

There are challenges to being an MP, but I enjoyed constituency work for the most part. I was pleased to discover that the letters 'MP' can come in very useful. People may say that no one respects politicians any more, but even now it does open doors. If I rang someone up and introduced myself as 'Alf Dubs, MP for Battersea South', I would often get the information I wanted, or be put through to the person I needed to speak to quickly. It was satisfying to be able to solve problems far more easily.

When I was in the Commons, MPs still had the power to delay the removal of immigrants and refugees, on the basis that time was needed to make further representations to the immigration minister. I could ring up the Home Office and say, 'Could we please not remove Mr X while I make further enquiries?' Quite often, when friends of people under threat of deportation could not get hold of their own MP, they asked me to help. Perhaps because I was easily available, and perhaps because I was the shadow immigration minister. It is a power that has now been largely taken away, but it worked at the time.

On one occasion, my wife Ann and I were enjoying a walking holiday over a bank holiday weekend, while staying at a pub in Malham in North Yorkshire. After a day's walking, there was a phone call for me downstairs. I was asked to call the Home Office to stop someone's removal the following day. This was before we had mobile phones, and I did not want to have a sensitive telephone conversation in earshot of people in the bar. So, Ann and I assembled all our coins and at 7 a.m. the next morning, and I used a phone box in the village to speak to the duty officer in the Home Office, who offered to call me back. Fortunately, I managed to have a stop put on the removal.

One never knew who was going to walk through the door during a constituency surgery. This made life interesting, but also rather hairy on a few occasions. One day, a large man came in and began asking for help. He then said that if I didn't help, he had a knife in his coat and would use it on me. I replied that I didn't think it would do him any good, and that it wouldn't do me any good either. He appeared to see the logic in this, but he then became a frequent and occasionally threatening visitor to my surgeries. I learned that he had a personality disorder, which apparently did not respond to mental health support. He was an interesting man who could intelligently discuss politics when he was not going through a disturbed phase.

On one occasion, I managed to get him into a psychiatric hospital. While he was there, I was approached by social services. Apparently, his derelict house in a well-kept part of Battersea was causing problems. The electricity meter was emitting sparks, and unfortunately it was situated near to the gas meter, which was leaking. The whole thing could easily explode. Social services asked me what to do and I urged them to switch off both supplies immediately to avoid a major explosion.

On his discharge from hospital, he came straight to my surgery. He was sitting in the waiting room when a newly appointed police officer thought he would pop in to meet his MP. He asked my constituent what he was doing there. Showing him the large hammer in his hand, he said that he was there to kill Alf Dubs. When he came into my office I could see he was agitated, so I asked my assistant to see the other people in the surgery while I dealt with the man. He was at least six foot four and very strongly built. He was also very angry. I thought it best to get close to him so that he didn't have room to swing the hammer at me. If he'd had a knife, I would have kept as far away as possible. Gradually, he calmed down. I arranged for a social worker to meet him at a nearby police station, and gave him some money to buy fish and chips on the way.

On another occasion, he was referred to a mental health hostel near my surgery. The director of social services phoned me in some anxiety to ask if I would be at my surgery that evening, as the man had just been evicted from the hostel by five police officers and was at large. Sure enough, he turned up. I was offered police protection, but declined on the grounds that having police hanging around would put off people who wanted to see me about their uncertain immigration status.

Later, I realised that perhaps I should have taken the issue more seriously. There have been at least two instances of MPs being attacked in their surgeries, in Cheltenham and Newham, and Jo Cox MP and David Amess MP were murdered in their constituencies. At the time, I believed I had the measure of the man and could talk him down, but that was naive. I was very lucky that the situation did not escalate.

By the spring of 1987 Neil Kinnock had brought unity and common sense to the Labour Party, but the Conservatives were comfortably ahead in the polls. Following her victory over the miners' and printworkers' unions, Margaret Thatcher had succeeded in bringing down further challengers to her authority.

For some time, the Greater London Council (GLC), chaired by Ken Livingstone, had been an irritant to the government and the right-wing media alike. It had ceased to exist on 1 April 1986. The Inner London Education Authority (ILEA), the body responsible for overseeing state-school education in thirteen London boroughs, went next. Whereas the GLC had combined excellent work building coalitions across communities with some silly policies and arrogant behaviour from its leaders, I believed the impact the ILEA had had on education in London had been very positive and I was sad to see it swept aside. In the Commons, I asked the Education Secretary how many representations he had received for or against the closure of the ILEA. The answer was several hundred against and two in favour: one from Wandsworth Council and the other from the leader of Wandsworth Council. This usually raised quite a laugh when I mentioned it at public meetings.

The Tories' strong position meant that many of us were expecting an early election. I was very concerned about my ability to hold my seat. The local party were as active as ever in Battersea, but there was no getting away from the fact that the constituency had been affected by demographic changes perhaps greater than any other seat in the country. I thought it was highly unlikely that at this election we would win the 'battle of the window posters' as we had in 1979. All I could do was wait, like everyone else, for the vote to be called and hope that I could campaign hard enough to survive for another term in Parliament.

The local elections were held on 7 May and saw Labour losses, leading many of us to think a general election was imminent. The next day, a Friday, I was in the Commons as the Labour front-bencher dealing with the private member's bills due before the House that day. The chamber was almost empty as most MPs had remained in their constituencies, anticipating the calling of an election. The previous evening, the Tories had said that they might pull the Sunday Trading Bill that had been slated for debate, but gave me no reason. I arrived in the Commons early on the Friday morning and checked to see what the second bill covered; it had the innocent title of Local Government Act 1986 but included a section about banning the 'promotion' of homosexuality by councils and schools.

I was dismayed that the whips hadn't picked up on this and ensured that the appropriate front-bencher was there to debate it. The bill was now in its final stages – the previous week, the Labour whips had allowed its second reading to go through uncontested, or 'on the nod', when one voice saying 'object' could have killed it dead. It was, to my mind, a terrible oversight and unacceptable that something with potentially very serious and wide-ranging consequences could pass with no scrutiny or proper debate. I did not know what the official party line was on this clause, but I decided that this was a nasty bill and I would stop it if I could.

The AIDS epidemic was claiming many lives by this point. What should have been treated as a public health emergency had been turned, by certain sections of the media and some politicians, into a moral issue. This was the age of Mary Whitehouse and rising hysteria over what sorts of material children should have access to. This all fed into a backlash against the rights and recognitions that gay people had been fighting for and slowly gaining since the Sexual Offences Act in 1967, which had partially decriminalised sex between men.

I sent messages via the whip to the Labour Party Parliamentary Office that it was important that the front-bencher dealing with the Local Government Bill should be ready at short notice, but there was no sign anyone was going to turn up. My only option was to effectively filibuster – to keep talking and prolong the debate until we were out of time. As there was not a single amendment down, this was going to be exceptionally difficult.

The debate started and every time the Tories wanted to give way for my contribution I sat still, hoping that reinforcements would arrive. Then, when everyone had spoken, I had to get up. Had I been given advance warning, I could have prepared something, but talking about homosexuality and education off the cuff did not seem to be all that easy. Somehow I kept on going, annoying the Tories who occasionally interrupted me. Each time they did I was relieved as it gave me a little more time to think.

Dame Jill Knight, the Conservative back-bencher who was a proponent of the bill, was clearly conflating education about sexuality with the spread of AIDS. Her argument was that 'that little children as young as five years of age in our schools ought not to be taught that homosexuality is a normal way of life', not least because it was 'undoubtedly true that the desperate disease of AIDS starts with and comes mainly from homosexuals'.

My counterargument, which I made again and again to buy time, was that AIDS did not just affect the homosexual community; that the bill should never have gone through on the nod without proper scrutiny; and that – most importantly – such woolly legislation could prevent young people receiving information that they needed for their health and well-being. Not least about how to protect themselves from contracting HIV.

After what seemed a very long time, I felt my speech had to come to an end as I was busy repeating myself on parliamentary procedures, lack of proper scrutiny of an important bill, civil liberties, HIV and AIDS and anything else I could think of. During one Tory interruption I whispered to our whip, Frank Haynes, that I had run out of things to say and proposed calling a division.

This is where understanding parliamentary procedure is very useful. For a division (vote) to succeed, there must be thirty-five members voting, plus four tellers (two to count the 'ayes' and two the 'noes'), plus the Speaker, making a total of forty. If there are insufficient numbers voting, the motion fails. Frank's job was to stand outside one of the lobbies and stop any Labour member from voting at all, and I would do the same at the entrance to the other lobby. The division bells went and several Labour members who had not been in the chamber appeared asking what it was all about. I said to Denis Healey, 'Please just go away and have a coffee for socialism!' The result was 27:0, which meant that the bill had failed. Had the result been 35:0, it would have passed.

Three days later Margaret Thatcher called the general election. For now, the bill had been defeated. But there seemed to be no doubt it would be brought back in another way after the election. The newspapers were full of the fact that I had stopped the bill. My agent, Ann Creighton, was a bit taken aback at the implications for what was already going to be a difficult election campaign in Battersea, especially because of the demographic changes. Hate mail began coming in from all over the world, although there were also a couple of supportive letters from gay groups. That week, with the election now in full swing, Wandsworth Council had a special debate about my attitudes towards homosexuality.

The ban on the 'promotion' of homosexuality was eventually passed, in the form of the now infamous Section 28 of the Local Government Act, having been reintroduced in 1988 as a government bill. It also included a ban on local authorities distributing or authorising any material that presented homosexual relationships in a favourable light. Section 28 stood until it was repealed in 2003 in England and Wales and 2000 in Scotland.

Right: Baby Alf with his parents in Prague, 1934.

Below: A family photo from 1938, with a five-year-old Alf.

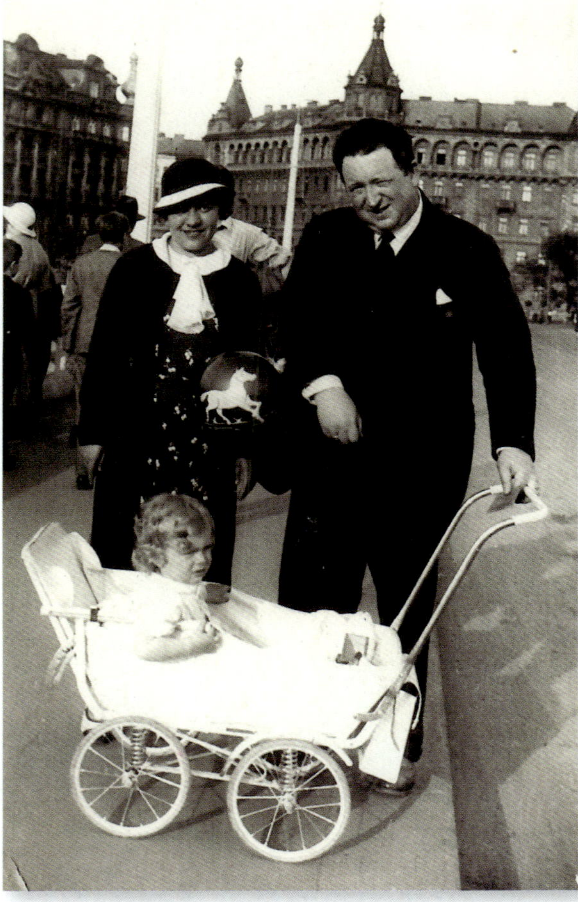

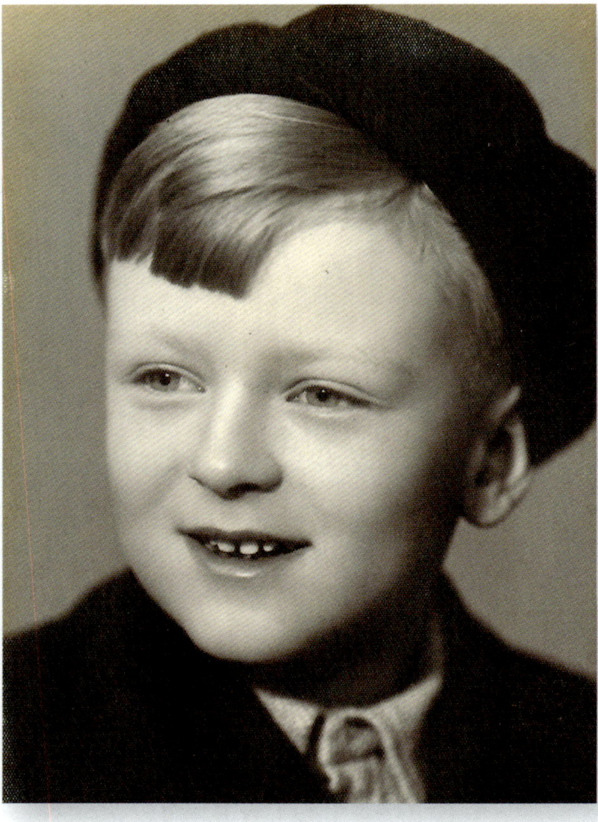

Left: 25 April 1939: Alf aged six, photographed in Czechoslovakia.

Right: Alf's Kindertransport disc from 1939.

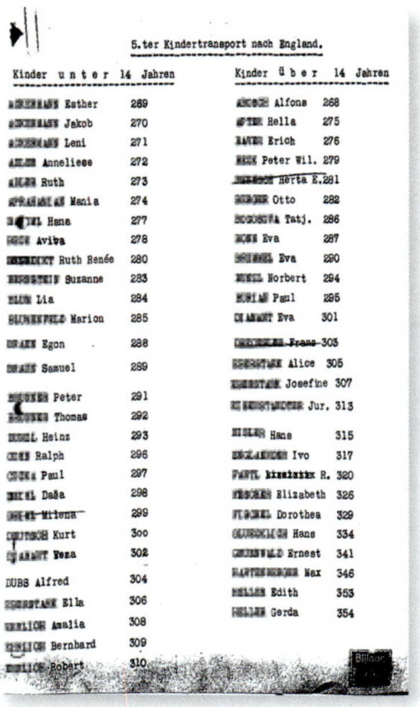

5.ter Kindertransport nach England.

Kinder unter 14 Jahren		Kinder über 14 Jahren	
[illegible] Esther	269	[illegible] Alfons	268
[illegible] Jakob	270	[illegible] Hella	275
[illegible] Leni	271	[illegible] Erich	276
[illegible] Anneliese	272	[illegible] Peter Wil.	279
[illegible] Ruth	273	~~[illegible] Herta E.~~	281
[illegible] Mania	274	[illegible] Otto	282
[illegible] Hana	277	[illegible] Tatj.	286
[illegible] Aviva	278	[illegible] Eva	287
[illegible] Ruth Renée	280	[illegible] Eva	290
[illegible] Suzanne	283	[illegible] Norbert	294
[illegible] Lia	284	[illegible] Paul	295
[illegible] Marion	285	[illegible] Eva	301
[illegible] Egon	288	~~[illegible] Franz~~	303
[illegible] Samuel	289	[illegible] Alice	305
		[illegible] Josefine	307
[illegible] Peter	291	[illegible] Jur.	313
[illegible] Thomas	292		
[illegible] Heinz	293	[illegible] Hans	315
[illegible] Ralph	296	[illegible] Ivo	317
[illegible] Paul	297	[illegible] R.	320
[illegible] Daša	298	[illegible] Elizabeth	326
~~[illegible] Milena~~	299	[illegible] Dorothea	329
[illegible] Kurt	300	[illegible] Hans	334
[illegible] Veza	302	[illegible] Ernest	341
DUBS Alfred	304	[illegible] Max	346
[illegible] Ella	306	[illegible] Edith	353
[illegible] Amalia	308	[illegible] Gerda	354
[illegible] Bernhard	309		
[illegible] Robert	310		

Left: The page from the Kindertransport list featuring Alf's name, 1939.

SPECIAL CANDIDATE ISSUE

Labour Life

Magazine of St. Marylebone Labour Party

Magazine of the St. Marylebone and Cities of London and Westminster Labour Parties

No. 251 JULY-AUGUST, 1969 Price 6d.

ALFRED DUBS FOR SOUTH WESTMINSTER

In our last issue, we included a 'stop-press' news item about the selection of Alfred Dubs as the Prospective Candidate for the City of London and Westminster/South Constituency in the next Parliamentary Election. Now, we introduce him to our readers in a full-length profile.

LABOUR'S new Prospective Candidate, Alfred Dubs, has packed a good deal of experience into his 37 years. With his wife Ann, and their two children, five year old Stephen and two year old Sarah, he lives in Westminster, and is Vice-Chairman of the South Paddington Constituency Labour Party.

He knows the 'Two Cities' Constituency very well, for he has studied, worked and lived here. Indeed, there cannot be many who have seen Westminster as a porter at Victoria Station, a student at the London School of Economics, a Civil Servant, and now as a Marketing Consultant.

Alf Dubs traces his active support of the Labour Party back to 1945 when, as a schoolboy following with interest the course of the 1945 General Election, he saw that the country's future lay with Labour. As a student at L.S.E. in the 1950s, he was Treasurer of the Labour Society.

Leaving the L.S.E., with a degree in Economics and Political Science, he went first into teaching, and then into commercial work. For a time, he worked at the Ministry of Health, but as a highly political individual, found the life of a civil servant frustrating, and decided to go back into commercial work, where he would be free to take an active part in politics. Although he is too modest for the thought to have occurred to him himself, others may wonder if, like other former civil servants he may one day find himself sitting on the Ministerial side of Whitehall's corridors of power, following the example of Harold Wilson, James Callaghan, Richard Crossman?

Alf Dubs' interests, aside from family and work, are wide. When he can, he likes to get away for quiet country walks. He is keen on youth work, and was at one time the Chairman of an experimental Youth Club in Paddington, run for youngsters who just did not fit into the organised activities of so many of the rather stereotyped clubs. He has been a School Manager, also in Paddington, and is an active member of the Executive Committee of the Westminster Community Relations Council, whose job it is to help the various communities in our City to live together harmoniously.

Members of the Westminster Labour Party, as they get to know their candidate more closely, are congratulating themselves on their choice. And they are confident that growing numbers in the electorate outside the Party will share that view.

ALFRED DUBS

Labour Life

Magazine of the St. Marylebone and Cities of London and Westminster Labour Parties

No. 259 JUNE 1970 Price 6d

Labour Life featuring Alfred Dubs as a political candidate in July 1969, and 1970.

On Clapham Common in 1978.

© Sarah Wyld

Above: Alf campaigning in Northcote Market in 1979.

Right: Former Member of Parliament for Battersea South, Ernest Perry, with Alf in 1979.

Left: As a newly elected MP talking to constituents in Balham, 1979.

Right: 1979: With Prunella Scales and Timothy West at their home.

Left: Alf and campaigners at the St James Hospital defence campaign demonstration on 5 July 1986.

© Candida Jones.

Left: 'Battersea in Perspective', a mural by Brian Barnes. The mural was painted in 1988 and depicts Battersea Park and some local heroes, including Alf in the bottom right.

Right: Alf with Sir Nicholas Winton, 2015.

© Philip Coburn

Left: Carlo Nero, Vanessa Redgrave and Alf at the 2017 Cannes Film Festival.

2018: At an event at Speakers House with supporting celebrities, organised by the United Nations High Commissioner for Refugees (UNHCR).

Alf speaking to schoolchildren in Parliament, 2018.

Right: Alf being interviewed by Jon Snow for Channel 4 while visiting the Moria refugee camp, Greece 2018.

Below: Alf being welcomed to a Greek refugee centre in Athens, 2018.

Left: Alf and his senior advisor, Candida Jones, at a With Refugees initiative campaign, hosted by the United Nations High Commissioner for Refugees (UNHCR), 2018.

Right: Campaigning against Brexit in January 2019.

Left: June 2019: Vernon Coaker, MP for Gelding, and Alf at a Safe Passage demonstration.

© Candida Jones.

© Candida Jones.

Above and left: Alf campaigning for the rights of child refugees, 2019.

Right: Lord Alf Dubs signs the Holocaust Educational Trust Book of Commitment in January 2020, marking 75 years since the liberation of concentration camps at the end of WWII.

Alf (*third from the left*) and Gary Lineker (*back centre*) at a refugee football training session in Fullham Football Club, organised by Hammersmith & Fulham Council in early March 2020.

Gary Lineker and Alf after the football training session for refugees, 2020.

© Candida Jones.

Above: 2020: At the Kara Tepe refugee camp in Greece.

Above: Raising awareness for refugees with Little Amal, 2021.

Above: With Sadiq Khan at the Iftar in Trafalgar Square, May 2022.

Above: Alf with a therapy dog during his recovery in January 2023.

Alf's belated 90th birthday party, May 2023:

John O'Farrell making everyone laugh at Alf's 90th birthday party, 2023.

Right: Alf at his 90th birthday party, holding a note he was sent in the post.

© Philip Coburn.

Above: Visiting the Holocaust Memorial Statue in Liverpool Street station in July 2023.

Right: Lord Dubs at the premier of One Life, the remarkable true story of Nicky Winton.

Alf with refugees in Calais, 2023.

Lauren Laverne welcomes Alf on Desert Island Discs in June 2025.

Alf with Irish President Catherine Connolly and Irish Ambassador to the UK, Martin Fraser, in 2026.

Part Three

LIFE PEER

I.

It's a depressing experience to lose your parliamentary seat. There is no use in pretending that losing is anything other than awful. From being at the centre of political activity, one finds oneself out in the cold.

There is a very good book that entertainingly describes what the grassroots Labour Party was like in the 1980s, called *Things Can Only Get Better* by the writer John O'Farrell. John was an active member in Battersea when I was the MP. One day, he approached me to ask me whether I needed any help in Parliament. I did, but I had to explain that I did not have any money with which to pay him. Instead, John became an unpaid researcher, and a brilliant one at that.

Though he was embarrassingly kind about me, John left things out of his book that would have reflected well on himself, for he was too modest. As an opposition front-bencher in 1987, I was responsible for handling a government bill on fire safety. I wanted to put down some amendments at the report stage and asked John to work on them. He spoke to the Fire Service, the Fire Brigades Union and the National Union of Tailors and Garment Workers – the last of which mentioned being concerned about fire safety in sweatshops. John came back with four amendments to the bill, and the government was persuaded to accept three of them. After I lost my seat, the journal of the FBU, *Fire Fighter*, published an article thanking me for these amendments. I felt embarrassed as it was John who should have been given the credit; it was an example of his political skill and intelligence.

I had of course very much hoped to win, and volunteers from the local party worked as hard as ever, but as we got nearer to polling day, our odds didn't feel good to me. Canvassing showed what we already knew: that by then there were fewer Labour voters than ever in Battersea. At the count, all I could do was watch the bundles of votes for the Conservative candidate, John Bowis, pile up, while the votes for Labour lagged sadly behind. The writing was on the wall, and the results were called at around 3 or 4 a.m. I trundled off home to bed.

The next morning, I travelled to Westminster with some bags and cleared out my office in Parliament with the help of John O'Farrell, who of course had now lost his very part-time job. Then I had to go to the Fees Office in the Commons and sort out the financial arrangements. My salary stopped on polling day, but I was entitled to six months' severance, around £9,000. Also in the Fees Office was Enoch Powell, who had also lost his seat in that election. I put party politics aside and spoke to him, acknowledging his departure from public life. He said that he felt it was much worse for me, because I was a lot younger. There was something slightly surreal about this conversation, given that until the election, I had been the shadow minister for race, community relations and immigration. And here I was, sitting with the person whose beliefs were famously totally antithetical to mine, but both of us had lost.

In addition to my six months' severance pay, as a former MP, I was granted £3,000 as a winding-up allowance, with which I was able to pay Kate Jessop, my brilliant assistant, while we went through the remaining casework and other matters that had to be cleared up. This meant that I was both unemployed and, in a curious way, still an employer.

After that was done, I took all of my things home and wondered what I would do next. I had thought a bit about it, but had not come to any conclusions as to what life after Parliament might look like. Many friends invited me for consolation lunches or dinners, but in the end, things quietened down. I was left with time on my hands.

The following Monday, I signed on for the dole. On the form, I had to indicate why I was unemployed and in the little box I inserted the words: 'Not enough votes'. I claimed unemployment benefit from the previous Friday, the day after polling day. The official asked why I had not come in on the Friday. I pointed out that I had not lost my job until about 4 a.m. on the Friday morning. She asked why I had not presented on the Friday afternoon, then. I explained that I had spent the afternoon clearing out my office in the Commons. She refused to backdate the unemployment benefit to the previous Friday but advised that I could appeal the decision. Well, appealing decisions was something I enjoyed, so I did. I won, and proceeded to collect my £31.45 per week.

Ann was working part-time as a teacher, so our family had some income, but I was worried about paying the bills. Finding myself unemployed and with nothing specific to do was a novel and not very pleasant experience. I soon began to behave as unemployed people are alleged to by staying in bed late in the morning, and not going into shops in case I was tempted to buy something. However, I quickly realised that, with much more time on my hands than before, I had to do the shopping and cleaning. I loved listening to *Woman's Hour* in the morning and made sure I was at home for that programme, leaving noisy chores such as vacuuming until later.

Applying for jobs was hard work and somewhat dispiriting. Former Labour MPs were not the flavour of the month when the party was not in power. Eight years in Parliament did not make me eligible for the top roles. And yet paradoxically, there seemed to be a reluctance to hire me further down the ladder; you could be seen as a bit of a threat to the person in charge. I was in my early fifties at this point, which didn't feel like the ideal age to be looking for a new role in a different field.

I applied for over twenty positions and went to eight or nine interviews, but without success. In the middle of this, the dole office asked me to come in for a restart interview, and the official wanted me to attend a Job Club four days a week. I declined his suggestion as I said I was working very hard to get a job and completing lots of applications.

I did discover that putting 'former MP, now unemployed' on my statement was a good way of getting elected in progressive organisations. I had tried for years to be selected for the committee of Liberty, which I admired hugely for its contribution to defending human rights in Britain. This was without any success until I lost my parliamentary seat. This council of members meets several times a year to discuss and set the organisation's strategies, finances and general governance. After a while, I was elected chair, though my time in this role coincided with a difficult period. A small group of people on the executive seemed intent on changing the ethos of Liberty to the point where I feared that they might destroy the whole thing. Every executive meeting was a battle. My main responsibility was to keep the organisation on an even keel so that we could concentrate on human rights issues, rather than internal shenanigans. Happily, we succeeded, and in more recent years Liberty has been a very powerful voice for human rights. Later on, after years of unsuccessful efforts, I was elected to the Fabian Society Executive. As with Liberty, my statement described me as a former Labour MP who was currently unemployed. Perhaps it was a sympathy vote.

While I was still in the Commons, Amnesty had suggested that I might write a book on lobbying, to explain the procedures to anyone who wished to communicate with their political representatives and influence policy. I had previously lacked the capacity to act on the suggestion, but, as I now had time on my hands, I thought about it again. It seemed to me that Amnesty's concerns did not cover the whole of parliamentary activity, and that any book on lobbying had to cover how to influence legislation. So I decided to write a book on all aspects of lobbying that I hoped would be particularly useful for NGOs and people in the non-profit voluntary sector, while also being accessible to anyone who wanted to understand the system.

The publisher Pluto Press was interested, and I decided that as an act of discipline, I would be behind the computer at 9 a.m. in the morning and continue, with coffee and meal breaks, until the evening. This helped to keep me sane, as it was a major adjustment going from days full of constituency and parliamentary business to having few demands on my time. I wrote the whole book on an old-fashioned Amstrad machine with a black screen and green type. When I was eventually finished, I had to use the incredibly slow dot matrix printer that came with the computer. It took two days to print the manuscript on long rolls of paper.

Lobbying: An Insider's Guide to the Parliamentary Process was reviewed in the *Guardian* by Dennis Skinner, the *London Review of Books* and the *London Business Magazine*, among others. Ian Mikardo MP had just published his autobiography, so we had a joint book signing during a break at the Labour Party conference.

Pluto Press mentioned that Number 10 had sent a car round to collect two copies. I suggested that they contact Downing Street to obtain a quote to use on the back of the paperback edition. Pluto told me that they had tried and been unsuccessful. They said, 'We phoned Number 10 and they launched into a long diatribe, at the end of which they said: "No comment, and you're not allowed to say 'No comment'."' I thought that was brilliant and wanted to include the quote on the book's cover. To my amazement, Pluto said that they did not want to do that as it might offend the prime minister. Well, I said, some of us have made that our life's work.

After about a year, I did get a job, as the chief executive of a very small charity, the National Council for the Welfare of Prisoners Abroad (now Prisoners Abroad). We mainly seemed to deal with football hooligans and people who had been caught with drugs in places where that is highly unadvisable. We had little funding, and it was a battle to make it from one month to the next and pay all the employees. But I was very relieved to have something worthwhile to do.

One day, almost a year into doing that job, I was visiting the Home Office when an official asked if I was aware that the British Refugee Council was looking for a chief executive, as I seemed well qualified for the role. I applied and was very pleased to join the organisation. Before I started work, I went to the AGM of the British Refugee Council attended by the hundred or so member agencies. Lord Chitnis, the chair, introduced me as being about to take up the post and remarked that for the first time in the organisation's history, the chief executive would himself be a refugee. I believe I was able to show empathy when meeting refugees on a one-to-one basis, and my front-bench experience as shadow immigration minister and my involvement in various committees were very useful too.

Part of my role was to raise the profile of refugees, particularly in the political world. It was relatively easy for us to organise fringe meetings and displays at party conferences. Our reception at the Labour conferences was quite good; the more so as I knew many of the people there. Things were somewhat harder at Tory Party conferences. But again, the most difficult part of the job was keeping the finances on track – a common theme in charities.

Coincidentally, it was around this time that I received an insight into my own background as a refugee. One evening in February 1988, I got a phone call from my father-in-law, who said with some urgency that I ought to switch the television on. The BBC was broadcasting an episode of their television programme *That's Life!*, featuring an unknown stockbroker called Nicholas Winton who had saved many Jewish children just before the outbreak of the Second World War by organising Kindertransports from Prague. There was Nicky, sitting among those who were saved thanks to his efforts. Like the people who appeared on the show, and who also owed their lives to him, I'd known nothing about Nicky Winton until I saw that programme. One of the women who was there in the studio was Vera Diamantova. The paper record of the Kindertransport on which her name appeared was shown on screen – and I was amazed to see that my name was directly underneath.

Some months later, there was a follow-up programme, in which the whole audience was comprised of Kindertransport children, now mostly in their fifties. Some of whom I knew as we had been at the Czech school together. It was a moment I'll never forget.

I first met Nicky in person at his birthday party at the Czech Embassy in the 1990s. He was a delightful companion and passionately interested in politics. He wouldn't suffer fools gladly. I learned he had stood as a Labour candidate in elections to Maidenhead Borough Council in 1954 and 1955, though without much hope of success, as it was as Tory then as now. He was friends with leading Labour figures such as Nye Bevan and George Strauss and loved talking politics. Over the years, I met Nicky many times, both in his house at Maidenhead and at events in London and elsewhere. It was thrilling to meet Nicky. How often does it happen that you can directly thank a person for saving your life? I found it quite hard to believe that I was still alive thanks to this modest and unassuming man.

*

In 1992, the Refugee Council received a request from the Home Office to ask to start planning for the arrival of 4,000 Bosnians from the Serb detention camps. We were to do this jointly with the Red Cross. It was an unprecedented number, and a relief as these people were living in terrible conditions in what were essentially concentration camps, in many cases having lost family members. We only had a couple of weeks to arrange reception centres and other facilities for the first arrivals. Getting it done in time was a close call. We agreed we would make sure they were dispersed in regional clusters around the country, so that not all the pressure was put on London boroughs, and we set up reception facilities in Birmingham, London and Newcastle. Kate Allen, as senior director at the Refugee Council, played an important part in these arrangements.

In our search for reception facilities, I was told that there was an old people's home in Balham which had just been closed. It was ideal. Main services were still on, the place was furnished and everything was in working order. The chief executive of Wandsworth Council, Gerry Jones, said that he would talk to the appropriate committee chairs to make all this possible. However, apparently, the proposal was put to the committee chairs at a meeting but rejected on the grounds that there was local opposition. This was a real setback and very frustrating.

I visited the local church and called on various residents, all of whom assured me that they had no objections and that they would welcome helping traumatised victims of war. I went back to the council, indicating the strong level of local support and pointing out to the Tory council members that it was the Conservative government who had set up the scheme. But the request was still rejected. I was quite furious.

We managed to find a disused psychiatric hospital in south London, which, with adaptations, was suitable. We urgently needed to identify and train some Bosnian-speaking support workers for our reception centres as most of the refugees would not be able to speak English. Most of the people in London who spoke the language were Serbs, as Serbo-Croat was very similar to Bosnian. We trained these Serbs in housing support functions and were ready for the Bosnians. The first arrivals landed at Stansted airport and it appeared that half the British media were there to film the event. I made sure that the Bosnians were not harassed by the media and that only those who were willing to talk about their experiences would be approached. Some were clearly far too traumatised, while others were willing to talk and explain the awful things that had happened. It was a poignant occasion.

However, we did have a problem at one of our reception centres when the Bosnians said they did not want to be supported by Serbs, as Bosnians had of course been persecuted, tortured and killed by Serbs in Bosnia. It was a complicated situation. We hastily managed to recruit some Bosnians and trained them as support workers, and in the meantime stopped taking on any more Serbian workers. This caused consternation among those who felt they were rejected for roles because of their ethnicity. The newly arrived Bosnians understood we were doing our best and accepted Serb support, provided that there was at least one Bosnian supporting them as well.

In Newcastle, we arranged an open day at the reception centre and invited all the key stakeholders – local councillors, social services, doctors, faith groups, community groups, police and others. It helped the local community to have a better understanding of the Bosnians and to provide support.

An issue that was complicated for different reasons was the question of Vietnamese boat people. After the Vietnam War, following the fall of Saigon in 1975, many refugees had left South Vietnam, often in small boats, to escape possible reprisals from the victorious North Vietnamese. It took some many years to find the means to get out, and they headed for countries like Hong Kong, Malaysia and Thailand. Processing centres were built, and many were offered resettlement programmes in the US, France, Germany, Australia and Britain. Towards the end of the 1980s, the numbers of those leaving Vietnam grew again for a number of reasons, with Hong Kong as a primary destination. Many now came from what had been North Vietnam and were not refugees, as defined by the 1951 Geneva Convention. The situation was aggravated by some irresponsible US politicians who said they believed that every person from Vietnam was a refugee and hinted that if they got to Hong Kong, they could be on their way to California. This was very stupid as it clearly encouraged more people to leave Vietnam.

The Hong Kong authorities and the British government were offering a $400 cash sum as an inducement to help these people go home and resettle. But some of the Vietnamese in London did not accept that many of the people in the camps did not meet the criteria for refugee status and began campaigning against returning anyone to Vietnam. Meanwhile, the camps were becoming increasingly controlled by Vietnamese gang leaders, who made it difficult for anyone to approach those who wished to return home. In some of the camps, there were real tensions and serious battles. This was an impossibly difficult situation, plus there was pressure from the Chinese to clear the camps before the handover of Hong Kong, due in 1997.

I visited Hong Kong with Lord (David) Ennals to see what was going on. I visited one of the camps and asked where a particular woman had come from; she said, 'South Vietnam.' I asked her why she thought she was a refugee and she said her uncle had fought in the South Vietnamese army. Where was he? 'In South Vietnam.' 'Was he all right?' I asked. 'Yes,' she confirmed. I said that I didn't quite understand why that made her a refugee. She did not have an answer. But the majority at that time were coming from North Vietnam and had no obvious claim to asylum.

David Ennals and I then went on to Vietnam to try to understand more about the situation. We travelled north from Hanoi and even beyond Haiphong with a Vietnamese official who worked for the United Nations High Commission for Refugees (UNHCR). We wanted to ensure that those Vietnamese who had returned from Hong Kong were safe and not being persecuted. We had a list of hundreds of returnees and called on some of them at random. In all cases, they seemed to be well. If anything, the $400 cash sum plus the electronic goods they had brought with them made them the envy of their neighbours to the point where it might almost seem an incentive to go to Hong Kong. Indeed, we were told that some of those who had come back from Hong Kong became 'double backers', returning to Hong Kong to get the benefits once more.

The Refugee Council was badly split by the report that David Ennals and I produced, with some parts of the media objecting too, and it took a little time to calm things down. Some of the Vietnamese people who worked with the council's member organisations, and in some cases had been refugees themselves, insisted that we had been duped by the Vietnamese authorities, who had arranged for selected Vietnamese returners to give us a favourable story. My reply was that we had selected these people at random and that none of the authorities would have known who we were calling on. We simply could not say that everyone who made it from Vietnam was a refugee – they had to meet the definition set out in the 1951 convention as being in fear of persecution. This was and remains crucial. Later, a Vietnamese member of my executive committee, who had been particularly critical of our conclusions, asked me whether it would weaken his case if he went to Vietnam on holiday. I answered that it would.

Alongside dealing with various crises and urgent situations, which necessitated swift action and some improvisation, there was also the day-to-day work at the Refugee Council to manage. We organised an employment training scheme, advising refugees on how to get support, managed some housing and ran a children's home and an old people's home. The children's home was largely occupied by unaccompanied young people from the Horn of Africa. I met one of the inspectors from the Social Services Inspectorate of the Department of Health, who commented that this home was quite unusual compared to many residential homes for young people that he had visited, in that the occupants were all at college or at school, and nobody was lounging about doing nothing.

At that time, asylum seekers were not allowed to work until they had been in Britain for six months. Now, it is twelve months and there are complicated restrictions imposed on the type of work that can be done. I learned of one refugee from Sudan who was highly qualified academically and had been offered a job at the University of Birmingham. He was not allowed to work for six months, so he spent the time twiddling his thumbs while the university left a vacancy unfilled. I don't know who benefitted from this nonsense.

About 60–80 per cent of Refugee Council employees were themselves refugees from many different countries. The day-to-day management of our staff of some two hundred in

Vauxhall and Brixton was complicated, but we were quite a happy organisation. Our member agencies with whom we worked included the main development agencies such as Oxfam, Save the Children, CAFOD and Christian Aid, as well as the Red Cross and community groups representing refugees from particular countries, such as Tamils, Vietnamese and Eritreans.

The Refugee Council not only had a focus on refugees coming to Britain but also on international issues. For example, while at the Refugee Council, I was asked to join a small international NGO delegation to the Caribbean to investigate the situation of Haitian refugees who had fled the country because of the appalling Duvalier dictatorship. Duvalier was overthrown in 1986 but Haitians continued to suffer from violence, instability and great economic hardship. We visited a few islands and I was taken aback by the hostility shown everywhere to Haitian people.

In a meeting, a senior Bahamian official boasted that he had ordered a boat of Haitian refugees trying to enter Nassau harbour to be turned away. I thought that this was a shockingly dangerous thing to do, given that it was well known that many of the Haitian boats were unseaworthy craft at risk of sinking. His actions might have resulted in the deaths of all those on board. He added that it was his belief that 'one more Haitian on this island and it will sink into the sea'.

Haitians who had managed to arrive in the Bahamas were locked up in jail, even though the UNHCR had assessed them as entitled to refugee status. The government then had returned them to Haiti, in a clear breach of the 1951 Geneva Convention. I then discovered that the only country in the region that accepted all the Haitian refugees was the United States. On the Turks and Caicos Islands, the US Army had established a magnificent hospital, should this be necessary in the event of larger numbers of Haitian refugees fleeing for their lives. Although, in the event, it was never used.

In 1994, I was invited to join an NGO on a visit to Myanmar (Burma). The object was to see if there was any basis for allocating development aid to that country, given the nature of the dictatorship. It was the only time in my life when my visa was granted by the cabinet of the country. In fact, I entered the country twice on that visit. The first time I crossed the border illegally from northwest Thailand with the authorities of the Karen people, who had an unofficial regime. It was just after the monsoon season and we went down the Salween River, which was still in full spate. The river at that point was the boundary between Burma and Thailand.

On the Thai side of the border, there were some hardworking NGOs helping refugees, especially the Border Consortium. This is an area with high rates of malaria and many of the people we met, including doctors at the hospital, suffered from the disease. But the work going on to support refugees was excellent, and the people helping in the camps deserved much praise for their humanitarian efforts.

We were told that young Burmese women were enticed

into prostitution in Bangkok and then forcibly returned when they became infected by HIV. It was despicable. One could not be other than desperately sorry for the young people who were lured to Bangkok with the prospect of more money than they could ever earn in Burma.

We visited Manerplaw, the headquarters of the Karen regime, and spent the night there. It was unnerving sleeping in the jungle in an illegal settlement. Not long after our visit, the place was captured by the Burmese army. We returned to Thailand and then to Bangkok before flying on to Yangon (Rangoon). At that time, the country was firmly in the grip of the military dictatorship. Many people had been killed by the army in 1989, suppressing the pro-democracy uprisings of the previous year, and the Burmese authorities had erected a series of structures to restrict further demonstrations. The roads had barriers in the middle, ostensibly for safety reasons. Given the lack of traffic, the obvious purpose was to prevent crowds from forming or moving across the road. Similarly, there were many overhead bridges or walkways, which local people suspected were there to give the military a vantage point from which they could shoot.

Aung San Suu Kyi had been detained in Yangon under military custody since her arrest in 1989. There was a firm refusal when we asked to see her. We were warned at the outset to be careful; if there was an event at which someone was very critical of the government we should not be taken in – this was probably a government agent trying to provoke others into making risky comments. I met one man from the tribal authorities who told me that after he was captured his leg was encased in ice before a white-hot poker was put on it. He showed me the scars. On another occasion, a doctor asked me to go with him to his office in central Rangoon to talk. Obviously, I was slightly nervous as I did not know him, but once there he told me how he had been imprisoned without charge, and his family left not knowing whether he was alive or dead.

At that time, there was hardly an NGO presence in Burma, but we met a Dutch man from Médecins Sans Frontières who was assessing the development aid situation. He took us into the garden of the hotel near the swimming pool, out of earshot of anyone who might be listening. As we sat by the pool in the twilight, mosquitoes swarmed around us, but we all felt the risk of being overheard was the greater danger. He was very critical of the regime and made it clear that any development aid should avoid investing in infrastructure, as that would assist the Burmese army.

We visited one of the senior directors of social welfare in his department. Interestingly, he and all his staff had been educated in the West. Popular belief in the UK was that the country was so isolated that there were few Burmese who had been educated abroad. I asked him a question which implied criticism of the regime and he gave us the stock propaganda response. Suddenly, his three or four staff members present burst into laughter. I was puzzled at first, but then realised that they were all strong opponents of the regime and that he didn't believe a word of what he had said. In fact, I discovered that he already had a post in UNICEF in New York and was about to leave Burma to take up the appointment.

One of the key issues in Burma at the time and even more so today is the persecution of the Rohingya. They are Muslims who have fled to Bangladesh, into the region near Cox's Bazar. Approaching from the Bangladesh side, I was told that there was something in the region of 100,000 people in refugee camps along that stretch of coast, most of them run by individual NGOs under the overall supervision of UNHCR. I visited some of these camps and saw firsthand that the Rohingya were in a desperate situation. There was little hope for the thousands of people stuck there, who seemed to have no worthwhile future ahead of them. It is depressing that persecution of the Rohingya in Burma continues, and today there are probably some 1 million Rohingya in that part of Bangladesh.

The hotel in which we stayed had been built by the Russians, and by the time I visited, my bedroom was very rundown. The bedside table was half broken, and three days into my visit the radio suddenly switched on, coming back to life. The bathwater was distinctly tepid and the colour of Irrawaddy River sludge. Standing in three inches of water meant I could not see my toes. Nevertheless, I had a clean bathmat and towel almost every day. On one occasion I was standing on the bathmat with an interesting pattern. I bent down to touch it and found that it moved. It was some form of insect.

Despite the regime under which they were living, the

Burmese were lovely people – friendly, gentle and charming. We could only wish them better days under a different regime. There is something haunting about the country, and I fully understand why some people fall in love with it.

Another issue at the Refugee Council was anti-personnel landmines and we campaigned actively against them. These were put in the ground in times of conflict. When it was over, they remained, without there being any record of where they had been buried, with the result that civilians would be killed or have their legs blown off. They could be farmers, children playing, people fetching water and firewood. Eventually, in 1997, the Anti-Personnel Mine Ban Convention (APMBC) – sometimes known as the Ottawa Treaty – was agreed, banning landmines and enforcing the clearance of places where they are known to be, but to this day millions remain undetected with lethal consequences. The campaign received a significant boost when Princess Diana accompanied mine clearance teams in Angola to raise the profile of the valuable work that was going on.

Altogether, I found the Refugee Council a most satisfying job. We were a multifaceted organisation working on behalf of some very vulnerable people to not only provide them with a safe haven but help them when they got here – usually arriving with nothing. Although the stress levels were higher than those of being an MP, the difference I could see that we were making for individuals meant it was more than worth it.

The organisation was invariably desperately short of money

and the biggest single problem was dealing with our recurrent financial problems. One of our large projects was funded through the European Social Fund in Brussels. I believe it was effective, but we were often many months into the financial year before Brussels would confirm that the next payment was coming. This meant that any reduction in what they gave us late in the financial year had a much harsher impact, as we had to give staff notice, and during that time, we ran up a bigger deficit. It was a nerve-wracking situation every year, and made managing a small charity particularly stressful. We fundraised energetically wherever we could, but somehow it did not add up to a dependable source of income. Ever since then, I have had enormous sympathy for managements of voluntary organisations because the outside world is seldom aware of how much time and energy is spent on simply making the books balance.

The role could be very political. From time to time, the government indicated their dislike of our campaigning and advocacy when it went against government policy. We then had to reassure the Home Office staff that expenditure in these areas came from our own fundraising and not our Home Office grant. During one European election, we produced a refugee charter, which was quite radical. Though some have since been adopted. Our Home Office contact said she was doing her best to stop the minister, Charles Wardle MP, from realising what we had done. In fact, many of the Home Office staff in London and in Croydon were extremely helpful and did their best to lessen the impact of some of the government policies.

The Refugee Council also provided teaching packs for schools about refugee situations in particular countries. For example, together with Oxfam, we produced a teaching pack about the situation in Israel/Palestine. Some US organisations received funding to scrutinise our work and report us to the Charity Commission if we stepped out of line. Oxfam were taken to the Charity Commission because of the main content of the leaflet. We were reported because the bibliography that we had prepared was allegedly not balanced. Of course, nothing happened as a result, but it took an awful lot of time and money to sort it out – a terrible waste of resources.

II.

At the start of the 90s, the Labour Party in Battersea needed to find a candidate to challenge the Tory incumbent at the next general election, which would have to be called by May 1992. I decided I would like one more chance to win back Battersea. I didn't feel I had been in the Commons for as long as I had wanted, and though I was proud of the work I was doing at the Refugee Council, politics was still very much in my system. I hadn't lost by much in 1987 and the overall mood in the country seemed to be that voters were getting sick of the Conservatives, which might allow me to regain Battersea for the party. Margaret Thatcher had just resigned, in November 1990, so we were waiting to see how John Major would get on as prime minster.

I put myself forward as a candidate and was selected. It wasn't a long bus ride between the offices of the Refugee Council in Vauxhall, south London, and Battersea Labour HQ, and most meetings were in the evening. I was once again juggling earning a living with trying to do something in politics. That's the deal if you want that life, and I didn't find it too difficult.

Parliament was dissolved on 11 March 1992 and the election was set for 9 April. The local party in Battersea mounted an energetic campaign as they always did, and there was a point at which I thought we might have a chance of winning. However, as polling day approached, it became clear that I was not going to regain my seat. John Bowis, the Conservative MP, held the seat, increasing his share of votes. Across the country, Labour came away with forty more seats, but while it significantly reduced the Conservative majority, it was not enough. Some have since blamed the party and Neil Kinnock for the defeat, saying he took an overconfident, bombastic tone at the Sheffield rally, held a week before the election. I didn't think it had any effect on the outcome, and I remained a big fan of Neil Kinnock.

After the election, I thanked the Battersea Labour Party members and said I felt that having lost twice, I was no longer suitable as a candidate in Battersea. Once you have lost more than once, that really has to be it. I was very grateful for their support and their loyalty and I didn't wish to push that further. I was disappointed of course, as I would have very much liked to have been an MP again. But perhaps less crestfallen than had I expected to win. Happily, I have retained many friendships in Battersea, am frequently in touch and often go back to help to canvass in elections.

Neil Kinnock resigned as leader and was succeeded by John Smith, almost unopposed. I thought he was a man of great integrity with good values, as well as having the potential to be a very effective leader. Then, in May 1994, came the shocking news that John had died suddenly from a heart attack. He was fifty-five years old. It was a tremendous blow to all who knew him and to the party. We were all devastated; I was in tears when I heard. I feel sure that Labour would have won in 1997 with John as leader. Perhaps not with such a large majority as New Labour did, but a very good majority. And I doubt very much that we would have entered the Iraq War under John's leadership.

The candidates for the leadership were Margaret Beckett – making her the first woman to stand for election as Labour Party leader – John Prescott and the shadow Home Secretary Tony Blair. Gordon Brown, the shadow Chancellor, decided not to stand. I like Gordon Brown very much, but I could see that Tony was more likely to win the election. He and Gordon had first entered Parliament in 1983 when I was still an MP, so I knew them a bit. And Tony lived in my constituency for a short time.

While the next party leader was being decided, Margaret Beckett took over as acting leader. Not long after, I had a phone call from her in which she told me that was proposing to nominate me for a peerage. It was not a complete surprise as I knew someone in the Lords who had been making a bit of noise about getting me appointed. I had been offered a place some years before, after I was defeated in the 1987 election, but I had turned it down as I thought that I should like to fight for the Battersea seat one more time if the party would nominate me. This was foolish of me because it was by no means certain that they would. You don't often get a second go, but of course I did.

I was very pleased that the offer had been renewed and I accepted with gratitude. I did mutter something about wishing there didn't have to be a title to go along with the position, but Margaret pointed out that there was no way around it. In the event, Margaret was only able to appoint three people to the Lords that year – the other two Labour nominees were Josie Farrington, former chair of education on Lancashire County Council, and Derek Gladwin, a senior GMB trade union official who had gained a reputation as a tough chair of the Labour Party Conference Arrangements Committee. They were both great socialists and colleagues. We were appointed at a time when the Labour Party had suffered twelve deaths and could barely maintain a successful opposition in the Lords with our depleted numbers and ageing membership. There was some talk that Blair's team thought that Margaret Beckett shouldn't be appointing people at all as acting leader, that it should wait until Tony Blair had been elected. Regardless, it went ahead.

I was at an event just after my appointment was confirmed and Tony came over to say congratulations. He made a joke that being a peer would certainly get me a table in a restaurant, at least. I countered that it would make no difference at all in the kinds of restaurants I could afford to eat in.

While I respect some traditions, I have always found the robes and flummery of the upper house ridiculous. It makes it seem like we inhabit another world. Every time the media want to have a go at the Lords, they show pictures of them wearing long fur-trimmed robes looking like a relic from another century. However, if a member of the Lords wants to attend the state opening of Parliament, she or he must wear them. While hereditary peers own them, for the rest, it is necessary to enter a ballot to borrow one or to hire them for a few hundred pounds from a specialist supplier. However, I must concede that the jacket with gold thread worn by the Garter King of Arms when she or he takes part in the introduction ceremony is rather spectacular. I have thought I should borrow it for the Glastonbury Festival.

I also don't like titles because anything that distances you from the people you are supposed to working for is unhelpful and unhealthy politically. Although I do admit that titles are often helpful in foreign countries, where they are less familiar with the British system, so being Lord or Lady someone can make people think you are more important than you are, which opens doors and sometimes means you can get things done. But here at home, most people don't like titles. They either make people unduly deferential or they suspect I am a bit of a nerd. Neither of which are a helpful basis for empathy or rapport.

The 'of somewhere' bit – the territorial designation – in the title you acquire when you join the Lords is not considered particularly important and is only really used to distinguish peers with the same name. Not that it was a problem in my case. As I had to have one, I decided that I wanted to be 'Lord Dubs of Wandsworth', partly to annoy my old adversaries on the Tory Wandsworth Council. But I was told I was not senior enough in the pecking order for that – I could choose part of a constituency but not a whole local authority area. I could have argued about this, but I was not particularly bothered about what I was called. Battersea was technically already taken – my old friend and colleague Douglas Jay was Lord Jay of Battersea – but this seemed not to matter when I suggested it. Although I have never heard of that sort of doubling up happening before or since. Douglas said he didn't mind.

Before the ceremony, in September 1994, I had a meeting with Ted Graham, then Chief Whip in the Lords. I asked him if I had to wear the 'Father Christmas' type ermine; some of my animal-loving friends had urged me not to. He said I had no option in order to become a member of the Lords, and that I had to do so as he needed my votes. So, I wore the ermine, and it was the first compromise I made when joining the Lords.

Being introduced into the Lords is an extraordinary, almost surreal experience. In those days, the introduction ceremony was much more complicated than now, and it involved not just ermine but funny hats. I was introduced by two colleagues,

Stanley Clinton-Davis and Fred Ponsonby. One must be sworn in, either while holding a religious text or taking a non-religious affirmation. I have long been an agnostic or humanist and have always affirmed in the Commons and Lords when taking my oath of allegiance.

My family and friends were in the gallery watching. The whole ceremony is made even more difficult as there is a running joke that Labour peers mark the new peers out of ten according to how well they do in the ceremony – whether you bow at the same time as everyone else and silly things like that. During the ceremony, the three of us had to go on the back benches, take off our hats and bow graciously. At this point, my daughter, who has a very characteristic laugh, broke the silence with a burst of loud laughter. As I result, I had to struggle to contain my own and nearly lost my composure completely.

On joining the Lords, just like when I had first been elected to the Commons, I found that I had no desk nor anywhere to put my papers, letters and documents, which seemed to be multiplying exponentially by the day, as we didn't use email then. I was carrying everything around with me in a suitcase. When I mentioned this to Ted Graham, he said he could give me a desk on one condition – that I became a whip. I agreed, and was given a desk in Old Palace Yard, across the road from the Palace of Westminster, sharing an office with five other colleagues.

Unlike in the Commons, whips in the Lords have

speaking roles and cover specific portfolios. Whereas in the lower house, the whips are mostly active behind the scenes, making sure that everyone toes the party line, in the upper house, they respond to questions at the despatch box if the leading front-bencher on the topic is not around and they need to be across the business of the House to make sure everything proceeds as it should. Being a whip turned out to be a very useful way to learn how the whole system works. Within a year, I was given junior front-bench responsibility for energy policy and some aspects of the Department of the Environment. I occasionally attended front-bench meetings of the environment team in the House of Commons. We were very short of people in the Lords, so anyone with some political background was put to work.

I also served on the European Union select committee and its environment sub-committee. The Lords had a particular responsibility for scrutinising draft European legislation and had six sub-committees to help in the process. The convention was that British ministers on the Council of Ministers would not agree a new policy until the select committee had scrutinised it and recommended what should be done. These select committees worked in the same way as Commons select committees, by taking evidence in writing and interviewing witnesses, whether in London, Brussels or elsewhere. This process of scrutiny was considered the most thorough in the European Union, something which was widely acknowledged by our European partners.

The newspaper publicity about the Lords tends to concentrate on times when a government bill that has been passed in the Commons is rejected in the Lords. Many of these are of course reversed in the Commons – the bill comes back and eventually it passes. However, we also get quite a few concessions in the Lords when debating amendments, though these are not much publicised. They have the advantage that once the concession has been made, the government must stick to it when the bill goes back to the Commons. The result is that the Labour Party, combined with others, had far more real successes in the Lords than seemed to be the case at first sight.

However, as Labour peers were significantly outnumbered by Tories, what with all the hereditary peers, we sometimes resorted to some creative tactics to achieve these successes. Or, at least, block some Conservative government legislation that we saw to be totally wrong. One option was to stage an ambush. This could mean calling a vote when there were few people attending the House, but making sure all our lot knew to turn up for it. Of course, we had to keep it quiet so that the whips on the other side wouldn't have time to recall all their people. That could be challenging as there was one elderly Labour peer who would walk around asking loudly what was going on with the ambush and when was it supposed to be. And Barbara Castle was known for always going home early, so if she was seen wandering into the chamber at eight o'clock that would rather give the game away.

Once, a letter concerning a planned ambush for the Monday from Ted Graham got leaked to the *Daily Mail*, where it appeared over the weekend. Ted called me and said that we had better call it off. But that would have meant spending the weekend phoning around my 'flock' – the group of members for whom I was responsible as a whip – and in the days when not many people had a mobile, this sounded like a lot of trouble. So I said we ought to go ahead. On Monday evening, the Tories started going home and our lot slowly started coming in. The Conservative minister leading realised what was going on and kept his speech going for about forty-five minutes while their whips tried to spread the word that there was going to be a vote after all. They didn't manage it and we won the vote. One of the Tories came up to me afterwards and said that he thought it was very bad form. When I asked why, he said that once the ambush had leaked, he had assumed we would call it off. It was all a bit of a game, but when you are so heavily outnumbered, what else can you do?

Of course, a certain amount of playing politics is inevitable and certainly goes both ways, as I realised when I put forward a private member's bill in the Lords (which works in a broadly similar way as it does in the Commons) to address some unfairness in the financial system which had been brought to my attention. The issue was that in the mid-1990s, many building societies were beginning to demutualise, following the Building Societies Act of 1986, which allowed these organisations that had previously been owned by their members to become investor-owned banks. This resulted in a cash bonus of £1,000 or £2,000 for their savers. The problem was that the bonus only went to the first name on the account. Typically, in the case of joint accounts, the husband or male partner came first and the woman second. This had the consequence that in the event of separation or the death of the man named first, the woman received nothing. The private member's bill that I put forward in the Lords to address this had a lot of support. However, the 1997 election was looming and the Tory MP for Gloucester, Douglas French, who had a marginal seat, got wind of it and put forward a similar private member's bill in the Commons, which had the full backing of the Tory government. My bill was agreed in principle but the government blocked it from being debated in the Commons. While the Tory-sponsored Commons bill was passed and then got to the Lords. Douglas French didn't ask me to sponsor it in our House, which, somewhat naively, I was surprised by at first, as he knew where the proposal had come from. The bill was passed, which was good news of course, but Tories got credit for this piece of legislation, even though it had been a Labour proposal. But that is politics. The MP for Gloucester lost his seat in the general election anyway.

III.

When I joined the Lords towards the end of 1994, there was a sense of optimism within the Labour Party that only grew over the next two years. Campaigning started well before the 1997 election was called. Labour led in the polls and the country seemed increasingly fed up with the Tory government, which appeared to be falling apart, plagued by bouts of infighting and revelations of misconduct by MPs who had to step down.

Of course, the outcome of the next election – which we knew had to be called by the end of April 1997 – was far from assured. The growing excitement was tempered by an underlying tension and a need to be measured in everything we did. And yet, while there was a strong feeling that we should take nothing for granted, there was something of a mindset shift at this time from behaving like a party accustomed to opposition, to thinking ahead to government.

In the run-up to the 1997 election, I realised that the Lords were not being mobilised to help. While members of the House of Lords regularly went out canvassing, though they do not, of course, have a constituency, there seemed to be no central system to connect those willing with local organisers who could use them. Considering that the Lords contains a pool of people who know rather a lot about politics and therefore could support candidates, it seemed a shame not to use this resource. So Derek Gladwin, Josie Farrington and I decided we should see what we could do to make sure our colleagues were able to play their part.

We were given a desk with telephones at Walworth Road, which the Labour Party still used; the main headquarters by then was at Milbank Tower. We sent out questionnaires to peers to ask if they would be willing to take part and how far afield they would be prepared to travel.

I have always personally enjoyed knocking on doors and have learned a lot through face-to-face contact with voters. You're not supposed to spend too much time chatting, but you do get into some interesting conversations which give you a sense of what people are most worried about. Sometimes you hear about specific problems which you can then pass on to the local MP, or you can explain to the constituent how to approach their local council. Occasionally, you encounter people who are angry, but far less often than you might think. I have found that if you are campaigning outside of an election, people will ask, 'What are you doing here?', and if an election has been called, they will say, 'We only ever see you when you want our vote.'

Most of our colleagues to whom we sent questionnaires responded positively. I was initially surprised by the small amount of reluctance we encountered, but I realised that those who had been appointed to the Lords from a background other than politics may never have canvassed before and possibly found the idea of it somewhat daunting, or perhaps simply unappealing. I have a memory of leafletting with Lord Sainsbury outside a branch of Sainsbury's in Wandsworth, and he was rather more interested in observing people's shopping habits than speaking to the electorate. So, bearing in mind that not everyone had had their first experience of talking to voters on the doorstep in the early 1950s, I explained to other peers how it worked and reassured them that they would be sent out with a party member who knew what they were doing.

Another useful job that we in the Lords can do during an election campaign is to go out with new candidates who have not previously served as MPs. I have done that in other elections. The local parties always seem pleased when members of the Lords pitch up to help, but I don't tend to identify myself to voters when out canvassing.

Once the 1997 election was finally called on 17 March, all parliamentary business was suspended and we dedicated our time to helping mobilise all those who we could to support the campaign, which kept us very busy. Some colleagues were prepared to go almost anywhere in the country and worked extremely hard. One memorable challenge was organising a chartered flight of helpers to fly to the West Country to help Candy Atherton, who went on to win her seat for Falmouth and Camborne.

The build-up to the election on 1 May was tremendously exciting. Though I got the sense that those in the parliamentary Labour Party and their teams were tense and focused on guarding against any last-minute slip-ups, away from Westminster there was a real sense of positivity and engagement with politics which I could not remember being evident in previous elections. Sometime in the middle of April, I was sitting in the sunshine in a pub garden in Buttermere, in the Lakes, enjoying a post-walk beer, and it seemed all anyone around me was talking about was Labour and the election. Hill walkers are not usually known for being avid political commentators – many of us like to climb a hill to get away from the world – so the buzz of excitement was very notable.

On 1 May, I spent most of the day in Battersea, where Martin Linton was hoping to win back the seat from the Tory incumbent John Bowis, to whom I had lost in 1987 and 1992. Shortly before the polls closed, I had a quick drink with some Battersea friends and then headed to the BBC's election party to say a brief hello. By a strange coincidence I bumped into the Irish ambassador to London there, and we had a chat about the prospect for movement in Northern Ireland with a Labour government. Little did I know that I would very soon be directly involved in developments there. Then I made my way to the Royal Festival Hall.

The BBC had broadcast the results of the exit poll at 10 p.m., which predicted a Labour landslide. However, at the party in the hall, we were all eagerly awaiting the point at which Labour would cross the threshold of having an overall majority of one. We were all glued to the television screens until we passed this milestone. Then the party truly began.

It was an extraordinary night. When victory was confirmed, the room seemed to almost take off. I hugged Neil Kinnock and John O'Farrell, but kept one eye on the television screens as I was desperate to know how my friends who were standing were getting on at their counts. The atmosphere was like nothing I have ever experienced before or since. A bit of me wished I was celebrating as an MP. It was just starting to get light when Tony Blair arrived from his Sedgefield constituency to incredible cheers and made his now famous 'New Dawn' speech.

It's hard to convey the level of excitement we felt, what with Labour having been out of government for so many years and the country having endured so much under Thatcher. Someone remarked that in our lifetimes, even for the youngest of us present, there would never be a night like that. When you are in government, you must make difficult and unpopular decisions. There will inevitably be mistakes and people will get disillusioned. There would never be a night like that again. But as the day of 2 May 1997 began, it contained nothing but potential.

Part Four

MINISTER

I.

On Tuesday, 6 May 1997, I was at home, having enjoyed a weekend of celebration following Labour's general election win, when the phone rang.

I was not entirely surprised to get a phone call from Number 10, as ministerial appointments were being announced and I'd had a hint from Denis Carter, the newly appointed Labour Chief Whip in the Lords, that I might be appointed his deputy. I was, however, rather surprised by what came next.

After I had congratulated Tony Blair on his great victory, he said that he wanted me to go to Northern Ireland as a junior minister. Perhaps linked to my time there as a child, I had long been interested in Northern Ireland. Throughout my time in the Commons, I went there on various visits. It seems that Tony had been made aware that I had the background knowledge to take on a role there in a very sensitive time in the region's history. I didn't hesitate before saying yes.

The ceasefire that had been agreed in October 1994, and which had been a cause for much optimism, had been broken dramatically when the IRA detonated a bomb in London's Docklands in early 1996, killing two people and injuring many. The prospect of lasting peace seemed remote at this time, but a new government offered the opportunity for something of a clean slate for negations, and Tony Blair made a commitment to peace talks with the aim that power would be handed over to a devolved Northern Ireland assembly, with the different groups all represented. Ireland too had a new Taoiseach in Bertie Ahern, which added to the sense of new beginnings.

Standing next to me, Ann burst into tears when I accepted the appointment. She was very worried about my safety and was imagining all sorts of dangers. I reassured her that I would be looked after and that we were going to have a peace process. All would be well.

Very soon after the call from Tony, Mo Mowlam, the Secretary of State for Northern Ireland, phoned. She welcomed my appointment and asked me what I thought of covering the environment and agriculture. I knew little about agriculture but this was clearly no time to be asking questions, so I said I would be delighted.

Mo asked me to get to Belfast as quickly as possible. In fact, there was an event at the new Waterfront Hall in Belfast that very evening, which Prince Charles would be attending, and it was highly desirable that I should be there. I thought

I had better pack a bag rather urgently. It had turned into an unusual morning.

The next person to call was Susan, who was to be my 'travelling secretary' – the private secretary who would travel with me, as opposed to the other private office staff. A car was on its way to pick me up to take me to Heathrow airport, she informed me. And could I make sure to pack a dinner jacket for a big event that evening. To my alarm I realised that the shirt for my dinner jacket was un-ironed, so I took out the ironing board and got to work, while continuing to try to reassure my wife about my new job. Quite reasonably, Ann asked me how long I was going to be away, to which I could only reply that I didn't know. It was at this point that my driver arrived to take me to Heathrow.

At Belfast airport, I was met off the plane by Susan and two close protection officers and shown to my car, which was armoured. I learned that I was always to have close protection officers with me unless I was in a secure zone such as Stormont House or Hillsborough Castle. I was taken straight to the Department of Environment, where I met one of my two permanent secretaries and other senior officials, and got into my dinner jacket in my private bathroom. Thankfully, my hastily ironed shirt still looked respectable enough. I was then whisked to the Waterfront Hall, a large new concert venue for a special gala night, with Kiri Te Kanawa as the main soloist.

There was a large crowd present with Mo Mowlam at the centre. Should I give Mo a kiss on the cheek? I wondered.

Or would this appear rather too informal a greeting for my new boss? After all, we were in front of the leading Northern Irish people who were there for the opening ceremony. But I had met Mo a number of times before, and of course she was well known for her warm and personable style, usually preferring a hug over a handshake. I opted for the friendlier greeting and hoped I had done the right thing.

It was a great concert with wonderful music. And, in addition, sitting in the audience in the darkened auditorium gave me a little time to try to process the fact that I had started the day at home in Paddington and was now at a very grand event in Belfast as a junior minister in the new Labour government. I felt totally overawed.

The concert finished and we were off to the impressive Belfast City Hall for a dinner. The police asked us to move out of Waterfront Hall quickly, following Prince Charles. I got into my car with my secretary, but the roads were blocked and we didn't seem to be going anywhere. There had been a bomb scare. I noticed there was a phone in the car and I asked if I was permitted to use it. 'Yes, it's your phone, Minister,' came the response. Ah, of course. While we were waiting, I thought I should take the opportunity to phone home and let them know I was OK. However, while I was on the phone, there was a loud bang somewhere nearby. As I had confidently assured Ann of my safety before my abrupt departure that morning, this felt like a case of poor timing. I heard the police say that it had been a controlled explosion –

of a suspicious vehicle, I later found out – so I kept talking, hoping the phone's microphone wasn't good enough to pick up the background noise. Luckily, it wasn't. Nor did they hear the larger explosion that followed – the heavy, armoured ministerial car really shook that time.

I said a cheerful goodbye to my family, who remained none the wiser, as the traffic started moving and we headed to the second event of the evening. I managed to stay awake through the speeches, though I was very tired. Eventually, sometime after 2 a.m., I was driven to Stormont House where I was to stay for much of my time in Northern Ireland.

The next morning, on my first day in in office, I was due at to the Department of the Environment. The DoE covered housing, planning, public transport, water supply, green issues and many other issues besides, to the point where locals tended to call it the Department of Everything. Because of sectarianism, I had the entire responsibility for planning, which had been taken away from the district councils. I was given what is called in the civil service my 'first day briefs' – essentially a presentation of the work of the department and a rundown of the most difficult issues currently being dealt with. This is when you find out what you are really in for. I was particularly concerned when I learned about the state of Belfast's Victorian sewer system, which was publicly owned and suffering from years of underinvestment. Apparently, the whole thing could collapse at any time – which was easy to believe when I was shown pictures of the horrific condition of some of the tunnels. It was going to be difficult to find money to fix it.

The next day, it was off to the other department I was responsible for, the Department of Agriculture and Fisheries. There wasn't much time for briefings, as I was scheduled to spend the day going round farms with Prince Charles. Agriculture was an area in which I had much less experience than most of the areas covered by my other department, the Department of the Environment, but as farming was one of the largest economic activities in Northern Ireland, it was vital that I increased my knowledge as quickly as possible. Prince Charles, who was passionately interested in farming and the countryside, asked me if I had to spend the day with him, thinking it would be rather boring for me and that I could have been doing other things. I hastily replied that I found such visits totally fascinating.

Later, I was asked by farmers how long it had taken me to have my first farm visit in Northern Ireland. When I replied that it was on my second day, I was asked what took me so long. They also asked me whether I knew anything about agriculture. Rather than admit to knowing nothing, I said that I knew the Lake District pretty well.

When you are a minister who has been given a new post, not only do you need to get used to your new brief, but the people working with you need to get used to you in return. Civil servants are understandably apprehensive about any new minister. In my case, the officials working in the two departments for which I was responsible also had to adjust to the differences between the new Labour and previous Tory administrations. Fortunately, I found the officials and all of the private office staff invariably helpful and supportive.

I discovered that when I arrived each morning, I would always be offered coffee or tea, which was very pleasant. However, after one taste of the coffee, it was tea for me. Eventually, I was asked if I didn't like coffee. To which I said somewhat ungraciously something along the lines of: 'I like coffee very much but not the stuff that you have given me.' The next Monday, when I arrived at about 8 a.m., one of the civil servants came in with a cafetière of delicious coffee. How privileged ministers are.

Another excellent benefit of being a minister was that officials could adjust, or even cancel, events in my daily programme if there was a problem with the schedule. This certainly reduced stress. As a back-bencher in either House, I'd had no help and it was sometimes quite difficult to work out whether to leave a meeting that was overrunning or whether to send a message that I was going to be late. In Northern Ireland, all this was done for me. This accounted for the surprised looks from people in London when I said that in some ways, being a minister was less stressful than being a back-bencher, and certainly easier than running the Refugee Council.

Soon after I was appointed, I was asked to attend an event to open a hotel which had received some government support.

Seamus Mallon, who was to become leader of the SDLP (Social Democratic and Labour Party) and Deputy First Minister, was to make a speech, followed by me. Seamus and I had been good friends for many years. He was an interesting man with a great sense of humour. I had first met him in the early 1980s at fringe meetings at the Labour Party conference. Then Seamus won his seat in a by-election in 1986, after the Unionist MPs resigned their parliamentary seats because they opposed the Anglo-Irish Agreement.

In his speech at the hotel, Seamus referred to the fact that he had known me for a long time. He recalled a visit that I had paid to the border area of South Armagh, then nicknamed 'the badlands' as they were known for IRA activity, while I was in the Commons. Seamus claimed that it was all he could do to stop me being arrested by the British army on the edge of the GAA pitch in Crossmaglen, a few miles from where we were in Newry. While his joke may have helped me with most of the audience, I could envisage the civil servants saying to each other: 'Who have we got here?!'

Years later, long after I had stopped being a minister, I was invited to an event to commemorate Seamus's twenty-five years of successful public life. The Irish Foreign Minister, Dermot O'Hearn, was there, as was the local bishop. Seamus had always had a difficult time from the ultras on both the Republican and Loyalist sides. When he came to speak, in his rather droll way, he said that on the gable end of the house facing his front door, someone had written in large letters

'Hang Mallon and fuck the Pope'. Seamus added that he thought he had the better part of the bargain. The packed hall collapsed with laughter, except for the bishop, to whom all eyes turned. His face went bright scarlet, while he tried to look as if he hadn't heard.

Not long after my somewhat breathless arrival in Belfast, on 16 May, Tony Blair came on an official visit and gave his first major speech as prime minister at the Royal Agricultural Society in Belfast. As he had recently won the election, the crowds turned up to cheer him. He said that the peace train was leaving and if Sinn Fein did not get on board it would depart without them. I was sitting a few yards away from him and realised this was a significant moment.

This speech gave the peace process a real shot in the arm and set us on the path to the Good Friday Agreement. It was a sign of Tony's commitment to Northern Ireland that it was the subject of his first speech, and from then on, he gave Northern Ireland more time than any prime minister had done before. In recent times, when people have been critical of Tony Blair and said he did nothing as prime minister, I have always responded that his contribution to the peace process was enormous and he deserves great credit for that.

Still, Mo had an almost impossibly difficult job ahead of her. I very much admired her no-nonsense style and the way she handled the different groups and personalities. She had a reputation for being awkward sometimes, which she probably was. Although I never personally found her difficult to work with. She was under a huge amount of pressure and it could be very frustrating to try to balance everyone's requirements and sensitivity. Plus she was ill – she had previously had surgery for a brain tumour, which wasn't benign, as she had claimed, and was still undergoing treatment. Though we were not allowed to discuss this. I had a huge amount of respect for Mo and she seemed pleased that she could leave me to get on with my areas without needing to run much past her.

Early on, Tony Blair discovered that most members of the Cabinet had never visited Northern Ireland and so he encouraged them to do so. At one point, things were going well in the peace process and more and more British politicians seemed suddenly keen to come over. A senior cabinet minister wanted to pay another visit, but Mo was not happy about it. She told me with glee that she had tried to call him, and on not getting through, left him a message: 'The bandwagon is full.'

With the government's focus on the peace process, Mo's dedication and the American involvement in the shape of the very impressive and capable Senator George Mitchell as the US's special envoy for Northern Ireland, it felt like things were starting to happen and a lasting peace was a possibility. The renewed IRA ceasefire in July meant that Sinn Fein could join the all-party talks, which felt very promising. It was an exciting if tense time. Northern Ireland was at a vital point in its history.

II.

The annual Hillsborough garden party was scheduled to take place a little over a month after I had arrived in Belfast. However, we discovered that it would clash with the first Northern Ireland questions in the Commons. After some discussion in our ministerial meeting, it became clear that we could neither change the date of the garden party, for which invitations had already gone out, nor could we move the Northern Ireland questions in the Commons. Mo smiled sweetly and said, 'Over to you, Alf!' So I was to represent Mo at the party, and above all look after the Queen.

Before the garden party, the Queen wanted to meet all the new Labour ministers, except for the secretaries of state, whom she had met before. So, we all went off to Buckingham Palace. It was a pleasure to have a look at the pictures that were not on public display. We were all introduced to the Queen and I was able to say that I was looking forward to welcoming her to Belfast the following week. As we were chatting to the Queen, she asked how members of the Commons could follow the Queen's Speech, which takes place in the Lords, given the limited space. They replied that they could do so either at the bar of the House or in their offices on the monitor. I don't know what possessed me, as I did know that one is not supposed to address the Queen unless she speaks to you first, but I suddenly asked the Queen whether she had ever delivered a speech with which she disagreed. My ministerial colleagues looked appalled. There was a deathly silence, and eventually she responded that it had happened.

I thought I should probably behave with rather more decorum during the Queen's visit to Belfast. And, sure enough, on the evening of the garden party, Ann and I were given a two-and-a-half-hour briefing on how to handle the occasion. Many people from the community would be in attendance, including those who had done a lot of work for charities or performed other sorts of service. One of my challenges was to introduce the Queen to people I did not know. Considering I had only recently been sent to Northern Ireland, this included almost everyone. I had the equivalent of a filing cabinet of notes in each pocket with each person's name, and just had to hope they would be standing in the right order.

Before that, however, I had to get through lunch. I was sitting on the Queen's right and she spoke to me non-stop through the serving of two courses. The briefing hadn't covered whether I could eat while she was talking, so the Queen finished her meal while I hardly managed anything.

I heard at first hand how well briefed the Queen was on Northern Ireland. No doubt this was partly because of her weekly meetings with John Major and, more recently, with Tony Blair.

Thankfully, I managed to successfully take the Queen around the garden party after the meal. Or rather, if I made any mistakes, I either got away with them or people were too polite to say so. And of course, the Queen handled the occasion with true professionalism and aplomb.

With that bit of excitement over, I settled into learning how to become a minister. Or rather, learning how to be a minister in Northern Ireland – which was unlike doing the job anywhere else.

The very first thing that one had to be aware of is that the two communities tended to use different terminology. For example, the Unionists speak of Northern Ireland, whereas the Nationalists and Republicans talk of the North of Ireland. Language is always important of course, but in Northern Ireland at this time, the smallest slip, stumble or misplaced gesture could get you into hot water, as I found out.

On one occasion when I visited Derry City Council, a predominantly Nationalist or Republican council, I really put my foot in it. I had general responsibility for local government and, as such, visited all the district councils. I found it interesting how quickly the conversation could turn from national, existential issues to something much more local. We could be in a discussion about the peace process, then I would suddenly be asked a question about the price of heifers. In Derry, I was trying to explain that nobody wanted direct rule from London to continue a day longer than necessary. However, my tongue slipped, and I said, 'Nobody wants the Brits to be here a day longer than necessary.' Oh dear. There was an outcry from the Unionists, who said angrily, 'We are all Brits!', and I had to back-pedal. As I left the reception, I could see that the Nationalists and Republicans on one hand, and the Unionists on the other, were still arguing about what I had said.

The previous Conservative government had managed the situation by calling the city Londonderry and the council Derry City Council. On one occasion, an Ulster Unionist MP came to see me to ask if I would change the council name to Londonderry City Council. I said that if the council voted for such a change I would consider it sympathetically, and hoped that would be the end of it. With the Nationalist/Republican majority on the council, the chances of that were slim, and so I thought this question unlikely to arise in the near future.

On another occasion, I received a very angry letter from Ken Maginnis, the prominent Ulster Unionist MP, in response to a comment I made on television during a campaign interview about road safety. Every day when I entered the Department of the Environment building from the car park, I saw a sign that showed the total number of road deaths to date. It was particularly distressing on a Monday morning to see how the number had gone up over the weekend.

In conjunction with my opposite number in the Irish government, we introduced radar speed checks and penalty points, and ran public safety announcements on television.

The campaign was launched at an event at Dublin Castle where I said there were too many road accidents, and while the Dublin minister could speak about the Republic, I was concerned with accidents in the North. I gestured in what I took to be that direction. Ken Maginnis wrote angrily to say that I had insulted his culture and traditions in my remarks in pointing my hand in the direction of Belfast to the north, and not using the Republican terminology 'the North of Ireland'. In my reply to Ken, I explained that I had merely been making a geographical point. I soon learned how deep sensitivities went, and the potential for even a small remark to be used politically.

Six weeks after I had been appointed as a minister, one of the Unionist politicians demanded my resignation on the grounds that about fifteen years before, I had made a comment supporting a United Ireland. Which was correct – I had supported a united Ireland at the time, when I was in the Commons. I was slightly concerned, as I was still new to the job, and so I chatted about this to Paul Murphy, a senior minister and my colleague in Northern Ireland, who said that there was no problem as it was then Labour Party policy. At the next meeting of Lords ministers, I explained that there were demands for my resignation as a minister from the Unionist politician and asked if any of my colleagues had heard similar demands, but none had.

But alongside the difficulties, there was a sense that progress was being made. Relationships were thawing, and conversations were happening. Sometimes humour was useful, and things passed off easily enough. Early on in my time as a minister, I was invited to the opening of a new centre for the West Belfast Partnership, a government-supported community scheme. I was told later by a Sinn Fein supporter that their policy was that British government ministers should not be invited to the West Belfast Partnership offices or similar projects in the Falls Road area. But for some reason, I had been. Bertie Ahern, the Taoiseach, Gerry Adams and Alex Maskey, who later became the first Sinn Féin mayor of Belfast, were also in attendance, and a photograph was taken of the four of us outside the centre. The photographer kept urging Alex to get closer to me. He commented that he had never been photographed with a British government minister and humorously grumbled that it would damage his street credibility. I laughed and replied that it would also damage mine.

Another, somewhat unique issue that arose early on concerned shaking hands with Sinn Féin. It appeared that the outgoing Tory ministers had avoided handshakes so as not to upset the Unionists. I went to an event where some of the representatives of Sinn Fein tried to approach me for a handshake and were kept away by officials. I raised this at our next ministerial meeting and Mo said we should use our discretion and not make a big issue of it.

A few days later, I was visiting Martin McGuinness's constituency in County Tyrone, part of his Mid Ulster constituency. As my car stopped at the pavement, some officials came to warn me that the Sinn Féin's Martin McGuinness was inside, as well as a battery of cameras. I had met him years before, on a visit to Ireland when I was in the Commons. 'Hello, Alf,' he said, and reached out his hand, which I shook without hesitating. Afterwards, I heard one of the photographers say to another, 'Did you get that?' 'Fuck it; I missed it too!' replied his colleague. Perhaps they had thought they would catch me dithering.

One of the serious problems in Northern Ireland was that the Royal Ulster Constabulary was almost entirely a Protestant force. There was a long history of mistrust between the police and the Catholic, nationalist community, who accused the RUC of everything from institutionalised bias up to corruption and collusion with loyalist paramilitaries. Later, as a key part of the peace process, Chris Patten, the former Tory cabinet minister and governor of Hong Kong, would chair the Independent Commission on Policing for Northern Ireland to investigate this and suggest reforms. After devolution, the RUC was replaced by the Police Service of Northern Ireland (PSNI) in 2001.

In late 1997, a tragic accident occurred in the strong Republican area of Twinbrook and Poleglass in Belfast. A small child crawled through a hole in the fencing, ended up on a very busy road and was killed. Sinn Féin immediately demanded action – in particular, traffic calming measures. It sounds reasonable – but in Northern Ireland, things were of course rarely that simple. The problem was that the police regarded the area as hostile and were therefore reluctant to slow down their cars to almost walking pace when passing through it. Sinn Féin knew this only too well and I felt they were using the tragedy to push against the RUC. Gerry Adams brought a Sinn Féin delegation to see me, and I said I would investigate it and see what I could do.

Shortly after this, I was returning to my office when I received a message that a Sinn Féin demonstration was taking place outside. We were told to go through the car park to avoid the demonstrators. I was a bit bemused by this and tried to find out what the demo was about. I guessed it was about the demand for traffic calming measures. I did as I was told and entered the DoE the back way, but then I reconsidered and decided I ought to talk to the demonstrators. Susan, my private secretary, seemed dubious and suggested we should seek advice first. But that would take too long, and I had made up my mind.

I went out of the building through the front doors, where I encountered the demonstrators shouting what I presumed were hostile comments – though they had their backs to me and didn't realise I was there. Susan announced that the minister had come to meet with them. At this, they spun round in amazement, not having expected me to show up. Their demand was as I had anticipated – for road safety measures. I explained that I was working on it urgently and asked who to contact for more information. I was given the name of one of the local councillors, went back into the building and the demo dispersed.

Shortly afterwards, I had a meeting with the RUC and explained the situation and the need to develop a tangible plan to improve road safety. They suggested some version of traffic calming measures, which would be okay for them. I then invited Gerry Adams and his delegation to come in for a chat and explained what I had in mind. They seemed pleased, except that Gerry asked if we could put some road signs up in Irish. I replied that it was the local council's responsibility and not mine. The local television station asked me about the situation, and I explained that Gerry Adams and his delegation seemed satisfied. 'What about the RUC?' asked the interviewer, who appeared to think I'd thrown the police under the bus to placate Sinn Féin, and was surprised when I answered that I had also discussed the traffic calming measures with them and they seemed happy as well. The affair was an example of how the Troubles played out on a daily basis, with seemingly local matters constantly invoking the wider conflict and requiring careful resolution.

There were also some things which were less fraught than I expected them to be. It was said there was tension between the RUC and the Gardaí of the Republic. I started to get to know my RUC close protection officers, and one day asked one of them how he would be spending his next off-duty weekend. He said that about ten or twenty RUC officers were off to Dublin to enjoy themselves. Another time, on a visit to Donegal, I was told about a joint project between the two police forces to provide holidays for children with disabilities. Although you might be told one thing politically, in practice, the situation could be different.

I quickly learned that although nothing was ever simple in Northern Ireland, a solution could often be found. There was to be a ceremony to mark the significant improvement in the train service on the line from Belfast to Dublin, called 'The Enterprise'. As responsibility for the publicly owned railways in Northern Ireland fell under the Department for the Environment, it was felt I should take part. The idea was that I would travel by train from Belfast to Dundalk, the first station over the border in the Republic, while my opposite number in the Dáil, the Minister for Transport, Energy and Communications, Mary O'Rourke, was to travel from Dublin to Dundalk. However, my close protection officers from the RUC would have to arrange to hand me over to the Gardaí to look after me once we crossed into the Republic. For them, the easiest way was to take me by car and transfer me to a Gardaí vehicle at the border. But I protested that I could hardly make a speech saying we had a terrific new train service and encouraging motorists to leave their car behind, while running the risk of being seen by the media getting back into a car.

The argument went up to the Chief Constable and eventually a compromise was found. One of my close protection officers would leave the train, along with both officers' guns, in Portadown, the last station before the border, while the other, unarmed, would travel with me to Dundalk.

It was a great occasion in Dundalk. There were children from Catholic and Protestant schools singing peace songs. I saw Mary O'Rourke approaching me along the platform. I was meeting her for the first time. I said to her that this is a great occasion, shall we dance? She replied that it was the best offer that she had had all day. That comment subsequently appeared in the Belfast papers.

III.

The workload as a junior minister in Northern Ireland was heavy, with a lot of travel, but the job offered lots of opportunities to make changes and was never less than interesting.

Ideally, I would spend the weekend in London and return to Belfast on Monday, remaining there until the following Friday. In practice, I often had to fly back to London during the week to deal with Northern Ireland business in the Lords, or for key votes when the whips demanded my presence. In addition to my two departments in Belfast, I also had to answer questions on all Northern Ireland matters in the Lords.

The peace process required a lot of legislation to get it through Parliament, not least the setting up of the Northern Ireland Assembly to make devolution possible. While there were four ministers dealing with it in the Commons, in the

Lords I was pretty much on my own with it. I had to be there to stand up and move second readings, answer debates and move or oppose amendments. There were at least three former Secretaries of State for Northern Ireland on the Tory benches in the Lords – Paddy Mayhew, Peter Brooke and Tom King – along with former Northern Ireland ministers. It was quite an informed and sometimes critical chamber, so I had to watch my step. I soon learned that any debate about a specific Northern Ireland issue rapidly turned into a debate about virtually everything in Northern Ireland. I had to be on top of all that was going on.

That was, of course, the case when I was in Northern Ireland too. All the ministers from our team were regularly doorstepped by the press. We had a weekly ministerial meeting, normally using video conferencing as some of the team might be in London while the rest of us were in Belfast. We would typically be briefed on the military and security situation as well as the political situation.

There were periods during which I flew back to London almost daily. If I was lucky, the whips would let me leave the Lords by 8.30 p.m. to catch the 9.50 p.m. flight to Belfast. This meant that I could get to bed in Stormont House by about 12.30 a.m., be in the office by 7.30 a.m. and then catch the 1.20 p.m. flight back to London. It sounds worse than it was; provided one can do this without thinking about it, one can do it on autopilot. And of course, I had a very good team looking after all the arrangements.

As the Secretary of State, Mo had her own private plane and, of course, if our journey times coincided, I flew with her. But I often took commercial flights too. Unlike in Whitehall, ministerial boxes were black rather than red, to avoid attracting attention on these journeys. And if I did fly on a commercial flight from Belfast, I had to be booked in under a pseudonym for security reasons. My secretary Susan, who travelled with me, said that she could be Mrs Hardy and I could be Mr Laurel. I thought this was very amusing, but the security people got wind of it and were not impressed.

There was a problem one day when I was flying to Brussels. The flight should have been booked in my real name so it matched my passport, but my team had become so used to using an alias for the London–Belfast flight that someone had mistakenly used it for an international flight. The staff checking me in at the airport were confused – why were these names different, they asked. I wasn't sure what to do, and I really needed to be on that flight. So I said, rather grandly, 'That's how it is.' Somehow, they accepted this, and I was allowed to board.

On one occasion, there was an important event in Belfast and Mo asked me to stay later to attend and speak. That meant that I missed the last scheduled flight, so the office booked a plane, which turned out to be the one used by the Queen. My secretary and I were on it, plus one official, and off we went, drinking some of the Queen's claret. Soon after take-off, one of the crew asked if I wanted to arrive ahead of schedule.

When I said, 'Why not?', the pilot put his foot down, and the plane noticeably accelerated.

Mo Mowlam was always based at Hillsborough Castle, while the ministerial team – including Paul Murphy, the senior minister below Mo, Adam Ingram, Tony Worthington and later John McFall and George Howarth – lived in Stormont House during the week when we were in Belfast. It was a pleasant enough place and we were well looked after there. Which was fortunate, considering our workloads. It also gave our team a chance to get to know each other better. One never knew who would be around, but we had some good conversations over dinner, sometimes with Nigel Warner, who was Mo's political adviser, and with some of the senior officials and senior security officials. We all got on, and there was a real sense of camaraderie. It was only spoiled for me by the fact that I seemed to have more ministerial boxes to clear than others, and often had to leave the discussion to work in my room.

This taught me one important lesson. It was about 12.45 a.m. one night and I was trying to finish my boxes before going to bed. One item for my attention was a letter to an MP; I wasn't entirely happy with it and wondered whether to write a note rejecting the draft. But I was tired, so I signed the letter and went to bed. Big mistake. The MP did not agree with my answer, and the issue snowballed and took quite a long time to resolve. I learned to be careful with what I signed late at night.

Once every four weekends or so, it was my turn to stay

in Belfast as the minister on duty, in case any issues should arise. One of the responsibilities of the duty minister was to sign extension orders when the police asked for more time to investigate alleged terrorist acts, during which the accused had to be kept in detention. Typically, the extension was for an extra forty-eight hours – nearly always to carry out more forensic tests on weapons and sometimes to interview crucial witnesses.

When a friend asked what it was like being a minister in Northern Ireland, I said that one of the things I had to do was sign extension orders. He could not help but comment that it was interesting that a former chair of Liberty was signing these orders, given that Liberty had long opposed the Prevention of Terrorism Act. That stung. In defence, I said that I had never signed an extension order to hold a suspect beyond ninety-six hours, as set out in the Police and Criminal Evidence Act. Applications for extensions were always put to me for what seemed to be good reasons. It was not long before the responsibility for doing this was transferred from a minister to a judge, and I, along with ministerial colleagues, was relieved of carrying out this function.

Other than the pressure to scrutinise any extension orders, duty weekends could be quite a pleasure. I normally stayed in a three-bedroom house adjacent to Hillsborough Castle so that family and friends could easily come to visit. The grounds were an absolute delight, with a lake, but I had to inform the security guards before so much as going for a walk. Most weekends, I had events and meetings to attend in various parts of Northern Ireland, but once they were finished, I sent my close protection officers home. If I forgot anything, I couldn't go down to the shops, but if Ann was staying, she could go. And the other advantage was that coming over to see where I was working put her mind at rest; Ann was less worried about me once she saw the security precautions in place.

All too frequently, people in Northern Ireland would ask me: 'What do you think of us here?' I put this down to a lack of self-confidence compared to the Republic. Belfast, in particular, had become so synonymous with the Troubles to outsiders that it was often all anyone knew about the place. And although there was so much more to it, it was a city that had suffered terribly over the years, both from the violence and the lack of economic development that came with it. But I had to give some reply to the question, and usually responded that if the inhabitants were all as nice to each other as they were to me, the problem would be solved.

I encountered good humour and wonderful hospitality on a daily basis, and particularly in my role as Minister for Agriculture. On my regular visits to farms, the farmer's wife would often produce scones and cakes, which were delicious and all too tempting. An hour later, I would be at the next farm, and again there would be a tray of scones. If I tried to demur, explaining that I had already eaten something, I was met with the protest, 'But I baked them especially for you!'

I was warned early on that it would take me only a few weeks to put on the 'Stormont Stone'. And that's to say nothing of the whisky that I was offered elsewhere.

One of the important lessons I learned was that when farmers were present, I had to eat that which was under most pressure at the time. This varied but for most of my years in Belfast there was a ban on beef exports because of BSE (bovine spongiform encephalopathy). Previously, 60 per cent of Northern Ireland beef was exported, so the ban clearly had a serious negative impact on the industry. However, the incidence of BSE in Northern Ireland was much lower than in Britain, so I made this point to the Foreign Office. The answer was that Robin Cook, the Foreign Secretary, did not feel this was an issue on which he should use up his negotiating position in Brussels.

Shortly after I was appointed, the Welsh Assembly chose its ministers. The agriculture minister was a vegetarian. Northern Ireland naturally had two farmers' unions and the president of one of them, the Ulster Farmers' Union, was discussing this appointment with me. I asked him how long I would have lasted as an agricultural minister if I was a vegetarian. He looked at me and said, 'You're not too bad a fellow. Perhaps two days.'

It was not just the wonderful baking I encountered on my farm visits that threatened my waistline. Every year, there was a major agricultural show at Balmoral in Belfast, organised by the Royal Ulster Agricultural Society. The Department of Agriculture hosted a breakfast at Balmoral at which I had to eat an enormous meal. After porridge, I was expected to tackle a plate of sausage, egg, beans, black pudding, potato cakes and steak. With the farmers watching like hawks, I had to make a speech . . . Later in the day, I had to give prizes to the winning livestock. After a few months in the job, I was up to speed with the main issues agriculture faced in the region, but I never became comfortable approaching a winning heifer and attaching its rosette.

Agriculture took up a fair bit of time, not least because it involved travel to Brussels, in addition to my regular shuttling about. The member of the British government who was responsible for agriculture – Jack Cunningham and later Nick Brown – would of course always attend meetings of the Agriculture Council, which were among the most important ministerial meetings in Brussels, so I did question whether my presence was necessary, not least because these meetings invariably started late and often went on during the night, and I had rather a lot to be getting on with. But I was persuaded by my officials that it was important to be there. I soon realised that my attendance was noted by the farmers (or fishermen in the case of the Fisheries Council) and that the media liked to report it.

While I was a strong believer in the EU, every meeting of the Agriculture Council tested this belief almost to destruction. On one occasion, at about 9 p.m., there was a break so that the ministers could have a closed discussion of the Common Agricultural Policy. I checked who was to be seated on either side of me to see if I was likely to have a good talk over dinner. On my left was the Dutch agricultural minister and on the right was a senior official. I thought that looked promising. How naive could I be?! I looked up and saw that all round the dining room were interpreter booths with staff in them. Over dinner, we went round the table with each minister presenting their government's position regarding possible changes to the CAP from a prepared statement. Jack Cunningham spoke for Northern Ireland as well as Britain. The whole thing took until midnight, when we went down for the full meeting of the Agriculture Council. It seemed a pointless exercise as every one of the prepared statements could have been circulated before or afterwards.

The fishermen in Northern Ireland were acutely aware of the annual setting of quotas by Brussels and on one occasion I had to meet a group of them at Kilkeel. In a room were about twenty fishermen, all hefty men, wearing T-shirts with short sleeves revealing rippling muscles. I had been warned that they were very angry, and I felt a bit apprehensive about being in this room with my close protection officers downstairs. However, they were extremely polite, listened closely to what I had to say, and seemed to accept at least some of the arguments.

IV.

As a minister, you inherit problems from the previous incumbent but you are aware that your time in the post will likely be too short to solve most of them completely. No one is a minister for long enough to develop new ideas and follow them through. Unusually, when I was posted to Northern Ireland, it was with a certain hope that I wouldn't be there for long, as if the peace process was a success, it would mean devolution and local ministers taking over my job. Yet, however long one is given in a ministerial role, you have no control over whether the next person will carry on the work in the way that you were intending to. And of course, you can't know for sure what all the outcomes of your decisions will be.

The terrible state of Belfast's sewers that had been revealed to me on my first full day in office continued to concern me very much. Obviously, the previous Tory government must have known about this but was reluctant to incur the expenditure to fix them – which was now going be high. I could not find any money to deal with it. Then I discovered there was something called the regional rate, akin to council tax, over which I had some power. I planned a ten-year spending programme based on increasing the regional rate by a small but noticeable amount. I went on a half-hour television programme to defend the proposition, much to the dismay and anxiety of my senior officials, who were worried that this cost to households was going to land badly. In the event, though, the interview went quite well, and I justified the increase as a matter of urgency on health grounds. I never did discover whether the Devolved Executive, when it took over, continued the policy or used the money for other purposes.

There was some talk of privatisation of water when I arrived, as, unlike in England and Wales, it remained mostly in public ownership. I had to publish a green paper (a government consultation document that outlines potential policies) on the future of the water supply and said to Mo that I would find it very difficult to justify privatisation. She said I could include a foreword stating that I personally opposed privatisation. That was somewhat unconventional, as ministers could not really hold private opinions at odds with official policy. Anyway, nothing happened, and fortunately, water remains a public service.

One day, I received a report from a hospital in Belfast that there was an increase in the number of babies and small children who had diarrhoea. The suspicion was that the water supply was contaminated with cryptosporidium, a microscopic parasite. This was potentially very serious. The parasite itself is not life threatening, but of course dehydration from sickness and diarrhoea is dangerous for young children and anyone already in poor health. Urgent laboratory tests were being conducted to see if this was the cause of the outbreak – but it would take forty-eight hours to get the lab results. I had to make a quick decision. Should we await the results of the lab tests and hope there were no fatalities in the meantime, or should we tell half the population of Belfast to boil their water? The problem was that an announcement that the water supply might not be safe would itself cause considerable anxiety. Did I have the right to potentially create panic without any scientific evidence? In the end, after much agonising with my officials, I decided to wait for the lab results. Everyone in my office had a worrying forty-eight hours. Mercifully, they came back negative, meaning that the outbreak of diarrhoea had been coincidental. Looking back now, though, I am not certain I made the right decision.

Planning was an area that took up quite a lot of my time, and in which the decision-making process could be complicated. Fortunately, thanks to my time in local government, I already had some experience in this area. I also quickly realised that it was difficult to make planning decisions without seeing the site. My predecessor in my role seemed not to have done this, but I insisted on site visits in most instances. The officials gulped a bit but accepted the argument's strength. I have many memories of wet afternoons standing at obscure road junctions in the middle of the countryside, looking at sight lines.

During the time that I was a minister, the economy of the Republic was growing – partly thanks to investment from the EU – and we were doing our best to help the Northern Ireland economy grow as well. During the Troubles, Belfast city centre had hardly developed at all. The city was divided not just figuratively but literally; roads that went between different communities were closed by gates in the evening. Anyone with money to invest took it elsewhere. It was clear that a sense of optimism among the people of Northern Ireland would be important for the peace process, and one way to encourage this was to promote investment.

The marching season, between April and August, when the Orange Order and other Protestant groups parade, always impacts the image of Northern Ireland abroad, in addition to the regular tensions and sometimes violence. On one occasion, some Americans wanted to investigate investment opportunities, and we had to ask them not to come in July, the peak time for the marches. When they queried this, we were forced to explain about the possible difficulties during the marching season. It seemed they then decided that Northern Ireland was not a place in which they wanted to invest.

Back then the most contentious area during the marching season was the Garvaghy Road in Portadown. In 1997, the Unionist/Orange Order demanded – as they always did –

the right to pass through this Catholic area. As I understood it, the chief constable advised Mo Mowlam that he did not have the resources to stop the march, so it might be better to let it through. It led to terrible riots and many people were hurt. Mo received much criticism for this, and I think she was quite stung about what had happened. The following marching season we were better prepared. When I went to look at the scene, it was clear that even NATO would have had difficulty getting along the Garvaghy Road, such were the obstacles and men along it. There were violent protests by members of the Orange Order and others.

However, the violence seen in July 1997 and 1998 around the marches was thankfully becoming rarer. With the situation in the region more stable than it had been for many years, more and more British supermarkets wanted to enter or expand in Northern Ireland. This presented a challenge, as although it was a good thing in some ways, it was also a real threat to the local shops and indeed to local suppliers who were often bypassed by the supermarkets' central purchasing policies. I frequently engaged in discussions with Sainsbury's, Tesco and others, urging them to do more local purchasing, and they did sometimes meet my request. However, it was difficult to shield small shops and suppliers from the effects of the proliferation of superstores. The retail sector in Belfast city centre, in particular, was fragile, and we did not want to do anything that would weaken prospects there. Of course, the more out-of-town superstores there were, the less reason people would have to go into Belfast, Derry, Armagh and the large towns.

One way the government could channel investment in the right direction was to use the planning system to prevent out-of-town expansion. I refused permission for a new large Sainsbury's at a shopping centre in Sprucefield, outside of Lisburn. Sainsbury's were very unhappy and threatened to request a judicial review, but in the end nothing happened. I was also asked to approve an expansion of a Sainsbury's store within the town of Newry. I was a bit concerned about the possible effect on existing small shops; however, all the shopkeepers said they would be delighted about a store that would bring more traffic into the town, so it went ahead.

A judicial review did take place after I refused an application from Tesco to open a store near Belfast City Airport. Our barrister said in court that the officials were at fault for not having given me the full documentation. But I knew I had read every word of the lengthy documents. I offered to go to court myself as a witness to say this was untrue and unfair on my officials, but was told it was too late as our barrister had already conceded the point. As part of the process, I had to sign a deposition, and the lawyers brought it to my office in haste because there was a deadline at the High Court. They produced a Bible for me to swear on, at which point I said I don't do that, I affirm. Consternation. These things didn't happen in Northern Ireland and, in any case, there wasn't time to get the document reprinted to reach the court before the deadline. That presented me with a problem. I agreed to sign, saying rather sanctimoniously that I didn't need a Bible to tell the truth, so it didn't matter to me whether I swore on the Bible or affirmed on this matter. In the event, the building of the new store went ahead.

I've always had a liking for historic buildings and was reluctant to grant permission for any to be demolished. However, I also understood that there were often practical considerations and that the needs of the local community were not always in harmony with preserving old buildings.

Just off the Falls Road was a Victorian mansion called Trench House. It had been used as a teacher training college for a time but had been left empty for some years and badly vandalised. The site was wanted for a new Catholic girls' school. I was also told that the budget for the school depended upon a quick decision about Trench House. The ideal solution would be to restore the former mansion and have it as a centrepiece of the new school. Unfortunately, I had not been given adequate notice of the problem and there was not enough time to set up the necessary fundraising appeal. If the project was delayed, the school wouldn't happen. I had a meeting with the local Catholic bishop who impressed upon me the need for the school. I expressed my reluctance and told him that there would be a row if I allowed Trench House to be demolished. He agreed that he would say publicly that he had pressed me very hard to allow the building to be taken down.

Accordingly, I gave the go-ahead and all hell broke loose.

A brick from Trench House was delivered to the Department of the Environment and a local community paper, *Anderson's Town News*, attacked me. Given my views on historic buildings, I found all this very hurtful. The last straw was that the bishop went back on his promise and refused to back me publicly. I learned a lesson about the need to protect historic buildings.

Helpfully, I became good friends with Dame Fionnuala Jay-O'Boyle, the founder and patron of the Belfast Buildings Trust. I also got to know Dawson Stelfox, an architect with a strong commitment to the environment and maintaining architectural heritage. When Coleraine District Council applied to pull down Portrush Town Hall on the seafront, presenting me with a report saying that the fabric of the building had been so exposed to the elements that it could not be restored, I phoned Dawson and put the problem to him. Shortly afterwards, he came back with a technical report saying that of course the building could be saved. Some Coleraine councillors came to see me just before the end of direct rule from Westminster and local ministers were about to take over the brief, and demanded that I decide within two days, before my job came to an end. I suspect they were under the impression that an outgoing minister would accede to their demand to demolish the building. I made the obvious decision that the building was to be saved. Some years later, an article about the restored building appeared in an architectural magazine, and I was amused to see a comment from Coleraine Council boasting that they had saved it.

Despite all these machinations, sometimes, as a minister, one can make a simple decision that has fairly immediate positive effects for a community or group of people, which is immensely satisfying. There was an active disability rights campaign in Northern Ireland led by an admirably feisty campaigner. At her request, we visited some of the parking places in Belfast and she pointed out how few were earmarked for people with disabilities. I said to the official with me that we must change that and allocate more parking spaces. It was decision that was in my power to make on the spot. That felt like a good day at work.

However, my limited time meant that there were a number of projects that I would have loved to have seen through but I could not implement. I wanted to have tighter controls on traffic in Belfast and to introduce park-and-ride schemes around the city perimeter, which would hopefully also have contributed to commercial regeneration. I visited an interesting such scheme in Bristol and also went to Edinburgh to look at their dedicated roads for buses, which were called 'green lanes'. I pointed out that green was probably not the best colour for some parts of Belfast, so they suggested an orangey brown colour – again, not ideal. Unfortunately, I was unable to take either of these ideas any further.

I always thought attitudes to equality for women were even further behind in Northern Ireland than in parts of England. I was at a launch event for some new buses, which had a platform that could be lowered. I said to the audience that this would be very helpful, both for people in wheelchairs and for people pushing children's buggies, adding that this being Northern Ireland, the buggies would invariably be pushed by women. Heckling was unusual in Northern Ireland, but there were some shouts at this. So, I simply said, 'Look around Northern Ireland and you will see that women tend to push the buggies, so men, you'd better get started.'

Mo was aware of the gender disparity and keen to do something about it where we could. Ministers frequently appoint people to a wide range of public bodies so this was somewhere we could make a direct impact. Mo said we should ensure that at least 45 per cent of appointments were women, but I couldn't understand why the figure wasn't 50 per cent. I was totally committed to this policy on principle, but for personal reasons too, as I had not forgotten how my mother had been discriminated against when I was much younger.

Back in the 1970s when I was working for Lewisham Council, I was asked to set up a Women's Rights working party. I had access to all the employee statistics on gender and race for the whole council, and found, as in so many organisations still, that at the lower seniority levels, women predominated, yet the higher up the organisation, the greater the proportion of men.

It took a bit of perseverance to communicate the policy of employing more women to public appointments in Northern Ireland. Officials would advertise and then bring me a shortlist of three names for each position. I was disconcerted on one occasion to be given a list of three men. The official's response was that no women had applied. OK, I said, let's hold the appointment and advertise again. The official said that it would be illegal, and I said emphatically that it wouldn't. It would be illegal not to appoint the best person, but there was nothing to stop us from advertising more widely. In the event, the second ad produced more applications and the official had the grace to say that an excellently qualified woman had applied. She got the job.

But the same thing kept happening. Once more faced with a shortlist of three men, I asked to see the other applications. It turned out that an excellent female candidate had applied, but I was told she had no public service experience in the last ten years. I asked why not, and the official said that she had been at home having children. This is how I discovered that most of the criteria demanded years of relevant public service experience. I pointed out that this meant only older men would ever qualify. I had the criteria referred to the commissioner for public appointments and the wording was revised.

There are usually things you are advised to stay away from as minister because your officials feel they are too complicated and little could be achieved. But I do believe there are two key things you ought to do as a politician, particularly one who is fortunate enough to be in government. One is to get on top of the day's issues – there is no excuse for ignorance. And the other is to have a guiding personal philosophy, otherwise one flounders.

I was particularly concerned by the situation of Travellers in Northern Ireland. When I understood the level of discrimination they faced and how that was affecting their communities' living situation, I wondered what could be done. Clearly, some Travellers wanted to move about the country, but many others lived on permanent sites with very poor facilities. A particularly notorious site was on the edge of Belfast in a place called Mona Road. I said I would pay them a visit, much to the alarm of officials, who said that ministers did not go to places like that. I insisted, and – when they got over their astonishment that a government minister had come to see them – I had an interesting chat with some of the residents.

In Omagh, I had visited another permanent Travellers' site which the district council had made available. All the houses were in good condition, appeared to be well kept and the general environment was clean and suitable for children. Most of the residents seemed to be in work. I asked the residents of Mona Road if they were aware of it. They said that they were, that they liked the Omagh model and wondered if something similar could be provided.

Fortunately, I was friendly with the chair of the Northern Ireland Housing Executive. He agreed that they would help with housing for Travellers and would give them a chance to get on the waiting list for housing. However, housing for Travellers had to be arranged differently so they could live together in their traditional groups. Years later, as chair of a committee on the British Irish Parliamentary Assembly, we did a study about Irish Travellers and Roma covering the Republic, Northern Ireland, Scotland and England, and went to Mona Road. The accommodation was less decrepit, and the atmosphere as a whole seemed much better.

That is not to say that it is easy to solve complex problems. In the case of Travellers, I have seen the most senior person in a group dominating others and preventing people from different groups from living on the same site. I have no control over that – but as a minister, I tried to use what powers and influence I did have.

V.

At the beginning of 1998, though the peace talks were progressing in some respects, the Ulster Defence Association, loyalist paramilitaries, had stopped abiding by the ceasefire, which threatened the talks. Mo Mowlam took the courageous step of going into the notorious Maze prison to talk directly with convicted terrorists who were influential members of the group. It was a gamble, because it risked angering those on the Republican side as well as looking like the British government was giving too much credence to the demands of convicted murderers. While many advised against such a risk, Mo decided it was worth taking, if it had a chance of saving the peace process.

This was very typical of Mo. When she first arrived in Belfast, it had been clear to everyone that she was very different from previous Secretaries of State. Some of the Tory Secretaries of State had worked hard for a peaceful solution, especially

Patrick Mayhew, but they were all rather patrician in their demeanour. Mo was very much a street politician, and her approach surprised, astonished and delighted many people. With the public, she was friendly and informal, but she was a no-nonsense tough negotiator, too. She demonstrated a good sense of how she wanted the peace process to develop, made many brave decisions and had an excellent grasp of the concepts at stake. Her gamble at the Maze worked: the prisoners withdrew their opposition and the talks went on.

It is perhaps difficult now, at a distance of years, for those who have not grown up or spent time in Northern Ireland to understand how entrenched those on opposite sides were and why they stuck to their positions so rigidly for so long. A major issue was the IRA decommissioning of arms, which you might think would be a prerequisite to the start of a peace process. The Unionists certainly thought so. But Sinn Féin leaders Gerry Adams and Martin McGuinness had to tread carefully with their supporters to get them on side, including those on the extremes, who also needed to be brought round if there was to be lasting peace. To disarm was seen by some as surrender, which was unpalatable. And who knew whether the peace process would succeed? The paramilitaries were reluctant to put their guns out of use before the peace process was concluded to their satisfaction, while those on the other side were reluctant to start it until they were. And that was only one of the first difficulties.

It is also useful to remember that while power sharing was

the immediate goal and the only obvious political solution to the deadlock, it involved enormous compromise on both sides. For the Loyalists, a Northern Ireland Assembly meant looser ties to London and maintaining a permanent relationship with their adversaries. For the Nationalists and Republicans it required an acceptance, for the time being, of the division of Ireland into North and South. Though the Good Friday Agreement would include an important provision for the possibility of Irish Unity in the future. At the outset, both sides had a long way to go ideologically in order for the talks to work, not least due to the resentment and anger stemming from their troubled past.

Not all of the paramilitary groups supported the ceasefire, and outbreaks of violence while the talks were ongoing increased tension. On 2 March, Senator George Mitchell set a deadline for the day before the Easter weekend – Thursday 9 April. He believed that there had to be a hard deadline, or there would be permanent deadlock. He chaired many of the meetings and showed enormous patience and understanding of the different positions, so his threat to cease to play a part carried considerable weight.

Then, two days later, we heard the news that two young men, Damien Trainor and Philip Allen, a Catholic and a Protestant, and very close friends, had been shot and killed by members of the Loyalist Volunteer Force (LVF) the previous night, when they burst into the pub in Poyntzpass, County Armagh, where the two men were having a drink. Seamus

Mallon, the SDLP deputy leader, and David Trimble, leader of the Ulster Unionist Party, visited the village and ended up walking around together. This show of unity and the huge public outcry over such a horrific act gave further impetus to the peace talks at a crucial time. An extension order to allow the police to hold a suspect for longer while they carried out forensic tests on weapons was put to me for signature, and I realised it was for someone who was being held in custody on suspicion of killing these two young men. I signed it.

The Irish government showed a high level of commitment. And none more so than Taoiseach Bertie Ahern after his mother died. Instead of staying in Dublin he quickly returned to talks with Tony Blair, when people expected him to stay at home and mourn. I always found Bertie Ahern to be a friendly individual, and his fairly easy, straightforward relationship with Tony Blair certainly helped at difficult moments. Bertie once greeted me with the words, 'You must be awfully busy.' To which I could only reply, 'Not as busy as you must be.'

Even the week before Easter, it was impossible to say which way it would go. The atmosphere was tense. One party walking out would be all it took to miss the deadline, and then who knew how long it would take to rebuild confidence and get the process back on track. For those of us in the ministerial team who were not part of the negotiations, all we could do was watch and wait for news. In the final stages, not even Mo was directly involved in the talks, which went on round the clock in the somewhat oppressive atmosphere of Castle Buildings.

I was duty minister at the time and I decided I might as well stay at Castle Buildings to be in touch with what was happening. At one point, I was alarmed to see Gerry Adams and Martin McGuinness walking along the corridor. There had been rumours they would walk out, so I said to them that I hoped they were not leaving. They reassured me that they certainly were not.

All of the parties in Northern Ireland were engaged, and there was a growing sense that everyone really wanted to get it done. That is, with the exception of Ian Paisley Snr and the Democratic Unionist Party, who had walked out of the talks the previous year. They not only opposed the process towards an agreement but campaigned against it, including leading protests outside Castle Buildings while the negotiations were nearing conclusion. In the middle of the night, during a snowstorm, Ian Paisley even tried to enter the building but was barred.

Our brief as ministers had always been to try to get along with all parties, which I mostly did, but Ian Paisley was an exception. He would attack me in public and then be charming in person.

Even after the talks concluded, political incidents could flare up all too easily. When we were preparing to hand over power to local ministers I applied for additional funding to protect police officers being rehoused. Somehow, the DUP got wind of this – possibly by coming across an errant photocopy of an application for funding. Even though the money was forthcoming, the DUP immediately held an emergency press conference in Belfast, saying that we were risking the lives of police officers.

It was an irony that Ian Paisley criticised David Trimble, leader of the Ulster Unionists for supporting the agreement, and then later, having undermined them, came out in support of the position that David Trimble had previously taken. But people aren't static, and he did eventually move on in his position quite a lot, from the man ranting and raving outside of the peace talks. He eventually realised that he was on the wrong side of history.

The negotiations carried on past the deadline of midnight on Thursday 9 April. No one had any sleep, and by all accounts the outcome was not certain until the last moment. Happily, by late afternoon of Good Friday, Senator George Mitchell was able to announce that the talks had reached a successful conclusion. However, given this was Northern Ireland, the Nationalists and Republicans called it the Good Friday Agreement, whereas the Unionists called it the Belfast Agreement. It was a moment of hope in a place that had seen far too much violence and fear.

Of course, there was still much to be done after the talks concluded. Part of the agreement was that it had to be endorsed by a referendum in Northern Ireland and the Republic. In Northern Ireland, 71 per cent voted in favour, while in the Republic there was overwhelming support at 94 per cent.

A historic outcome. I went to the British ambassador's residence in Dublin for a party to celebrate the outcome of the two referenda. Attended by Bertie Ahern, and many of his Cabinet and government officials, it was a great occasion, and wonderful to think about how politics had been used as a force for real and important change – to hopefully end violence and improve lives. I will never forget the great wave of optimism that people felt about the future then.

Legislation still had to be passed in Parliament to uphold what had been decided by the Good Friday Agreement. One very contentious issue was the early release on licence of prisoners convicted of terrorism offences after they had served two years in jail. If one had lost a friend or family member to a terrorist atrocity or sectarian murder, this was often a very bitter pill to swallow, and yet it was an unavoidable part of the negotiations.

Travelling to Westminster to handle the bill in the Lords, as I did with all legislation related to Northern Ireland, I had something of a feeling of foreboding. I knew it was going to be challenging to get it through. The result of it passing would be that some notorious murderers, including those who had tried to kill Margaret Thatcher and injured several members of the Tory Cabinet and their spouses, would be freed. But if the bill was defeated, even if the defeat was subsequently reversed in the Commons, the effect in Northern Ireland would be quite damaging. It was a moral and political dilemma which weighed on me.

The Tory leader of the Lords, Viscount Cranborne, personally dealt with the bill on behalf of the opposition. Towards the end of the debate, he made the final speech before I wound up. He said in effect that he hoped that I would not be killed by terrorists, which seemed a bit threatening. I merely replied that I thought I could look after myself. At any rate, when it came to the division, the bill scraped through by four votes. Two Tory peers told me that Viscount Cranborne's naysaying persuaded them to abstain rather than vote against the government. They also suggested that others had been influenced in the same way. Perhaps it reminded them of the gravity of the vote and the possible consequences if it failed. So it was really thanks to Viscount Cranborne that the bill went through.

A number of legal and procedural challenges with the potential to explode remained as we tried to sort through the aftermath of the Agreement. Another requirement was the passing of the Northern Ireland Act, which gave rise to the devolution of power to the Northern Ireland Assembly. This included the procedures for appointing and replacing the First Minister. The Act said that should the First Minister resign, retire or die, she or he had to be replaced within forty days, or the Secretary of State would have to call new elections for the Assembly.

During the committee or report stage of the Northern Ireland Bill, there was quite a lengthy discussion on this forty-day point. Several peers asked me questions about it and I was under a great deal of pressure to clarify. I did say forty days meant forty days, but felt a little uncertain, and added the words 'at least I think so'.

After I had left Northern Ireland, there were at least two occasions when direct rule was restored because the parties failed to agree on some fundamental issue. In 2001, David Trimble, the First Minister, resigned and it took forty-four days to replace him. The delay was caused by the need for the Alliance Party to register as Unionists so that they could provide the necessary majority to keep the Assembly going. Peter Robinson, then leader of the DUP, demanded a judicial review of the Secretary of State's failure to call the election once forty days had been exceeded. This was still at the time when the House of Lords sat in a judicial capacity as the Supreme Court. I was tipped off that the case was coming up, just as Parliament was due to go into its summer recess. I spoke to Peter Goldsmith, the Attorney General who was taking the case on behalf of the government, and said to him that if it helped the government he shouldn't hesitate to blame me.

The judicial review depended largely on the debate about the amendments. There is a convention that judges can use speeches from Parliament to interpret legislation – this is called 'Pepper vs Hart' after a legal case many years previously. 'Pepper vs Hart' was always thought to apply to second reading speeches by ministers when opening a debate and making a considered contribution; it had not previously been thought to apply to the process of attrition that can take place during the committee or report stages.

This perhaps sounds like an arcane or merely technical point relating to the minutiae of who said what at one stage of a bill passing through Parliament. However, had Peter Robinson won the judicial review, it would have invalidated all the decisions made by the Executive and the Northern Ireland Assembly covering the period when there was no First Minister. There were therefore plans ready to recall Parliament to retrospectively validate all the decisions made during the period, whether by the Executive or by the Assembly.

Although plans were ready for this recall, surprisingly the media did not seem to pick this up. It would have been most unusual to recall Parliament other than for war or threats of war. Fortunately for the government, the judges supported the Secretary of State by three to two, which was a politically an enormously helpful decision, although I wondered about its legal validity.

Violence did not stop overnight. On 15 August, I was at home when I heard that a car bomb had exploded in Omagh, County Tyrone. It was a shocking blow when there was such a mood of hope in the region, and more widely, for the future. Of course, not all of the conflict had stopped immediately following the signing of the Good Friday Agreement in April. There were breakaway paramilitary groups on both sides who were against peace and wished to continue meting out sectarian violence on their neighbouring communities. But the death toll from the Omagh bombing – twenty-nine killed and hundreds injured on a busy shopping street on a Saturday afternoon – was higher than that of any terrorist incident in Northern Ireland during the Troubles. This was largely because the bomb threat the terrorists had issued contained wrong information, so that the police were unknowingly herding some people towards the bomb rather than to safety as they tried to clear the street.

It was very sad and a huge blow to everyone's morale. In London, I asked if I should head straight back to Belfast but was told there was nothing I could do that weekend. The authorities in Omagh certainly didn't want politicians wandering around their crime scene, which was now largely rubble thanks to the size of the bomb. The Real IRA claimed responsibility and was denounced by pretty much everyone. The widespread outrage added even more urgency to disarmament and to seeing the peace process through.

Sectarian tensions were also still alive. David Trimble was attacked by his fellow unionists for going into a Catholic church, which he did in order to attend the funeral of a Catholic child who had been on a visit from Donegal to Omagh that Saturday. As the senior minister, he did the right thing by going to the funeral of a young boy murdered by dissidents, and I thought it was terrible that he was criticised. It made me think of a Catholic priest who I had once heard say, 'We spend so much time being Catholics, we've forgotten how to be Christians.'

*

The first elections for the Northern Ireland Assembly had taken place at the end of June 1998. The Assembly voted David Trimble in as First Minister with Seamus Mallon as his deputy. The Executive was chosen by the D'Hondt electoral system, a rather complicated system designed for places where you have to ensure fair representation of different parties in government. It essentially forces a coalition. The new Executive was to have ten ministers, plus the First Minister and Deputy First Minister.

Choosing ministers turned into a stumbling block, particularly as the Ulster Unionists were unhappy with Sinn Féin's proposed timeline for decommissioning – the term that was decided to be more palatable that 'disarming'. Various deadlines sailed past, and a feeling of limbo and disillusionment set in. Rancour between the two sides was increasing until Senator George Mitchell was persuaded to come back to Belfast to try to sort the whole thing out.

He again prevailed, and the formal handover date was set for 2 December. In the autumn, we began to prepare in earnest to hand over to ministers in the new devolved government. In the event, my two departments – Agriculture and the Environment – were divided, and it was decided that roughly four local ministers would take my place, which seemed sensible. It had been rather a big job for one person.

But before that, Mo Mowlam was replaced by Peter Mandelson as Secretary of State. Her style as a politician had meant that she had often sailed close to the wind with her tactics and decisions, though always in service of the peace process and taking calculated risks. On one occasion, Mo was invited from Belfast to see Tony Blair, and I said please make sure you come back. She said she would do her best and returned. But that October, she was asked to go to Downing Street again. When she returned to pack up her things, she said that she had fought this once and couldn't do it any more.

The Unionists had become increasingly unhappy with Mo, and David Trimble in particular led demands that she be moved. On one occasion, I bumped into David Trimble in Belfast, and he said something about having talked with my boss. I asked him when he had spoken with Mo, and he said rather harshly that he meant Tony Blair. He clearly had little time for Mo, and the Unionists began to be more hostile to her.

Years later I would ask people how they assessed Mo's contribution to the peace process and found that retrospective opinions differed. On the whole, Nationalists and Republicans would say that her personal influence made a positive impact, and without her, it might not have happened. They tended to agree that she had put her personal stamp on the talks and deserved a lot of credit for the eventual Good Friday Agreement. The Unionists, however, have tended to say that there was an inevitability to the peace process, giving Mo little credit for the outcome and claiming that her personal contribution was nothing exceptional.

Having observed Mo closely over the years, I am convinced

that her personal contribution did have an enormous positive impact on the peace process. Her unorthodox approach made her very popular, at least initially. She worked incredibly hard and refused to discuss her health. I felt at the time that she had not been given long enough to recover after the operation on her brain tumour before she became the Secretary of State. In fact, it turned out later that she had not recovered and was still unwell, but simply carried on regardless.

I am pleased to remember the occasion at a Labour Party conference when Tony Blair was making his leader's speech. When Tony referred to Mo, there was a spontaneous standing ovation. Tony, probably a bit embarrassed, said it was the first time he had known of a standing ovation for someone other than the speaker.

I held meetings with my successors, in which we went through all of the key issues. This rarely happens in government, but I thought it was very important in this case and I made sure that time was set aside to do it as thoroughly as possible. In the end, though, my time in Northern Ireland ended in a rush as I was recalled to London on short notice. I was disappointed as I did not have enough time to say goodbye to my excellent team, to whom I had, of course, become close during my two and a half memorable years in Northern Ireland.

At 10 Downing Street, I was presented with two letters: my letter of resignation to Tony Blair and his reply to me, thanking me for my work. I changed my letter to Tony and discussed it with his press secretary, Alistair Campbell, who was happy with my new version. Ultimately, handing over to local ministers was a success for the government. There was no better way for me to go.

It was strange to be back in London with rather more time on my hands than I'd had available for quite some time. But I was delighted to have played a role in that historic period. Ann was pleased to have me home, although she had enjoyed her visits to Belfast.

Of course, it has not been plain sailing for the devolved Northern Irish government, and during one of the periods when direct rule from Westminster was resumed for a time there was a chance I would be sent back, but it came to nothing. No one from the Lords was appointed, though some Tories suggested me. With my long history in Northern Ireland, I would have liked to have returned to Belfast, but you can't live in the past. You have to keep focused on the future.

I did retain my connection to Ireland and Northern Ireland through the British Irish Parliamentary Assembly (BIPA), which comprises parliamentarians from Belfast, Cardiff, Dublin, Edinburgh and London, as well as Crown Dependencies – the Channel Islands and the Isle of Man. A lot of the leading Irish politicians have been involved in BIPA, including some who went on to become ministers in Dublin. Soon after I stopped being a minister, I was appointed to the British Delegation and then chaired one of the committees on environment and social policy, which works rather like a parliamentary Select

Committee in the way it chooses which topics to investigate. I was pleased to have the opportunity to sustain my contact with parliamentarians and ministers relating to the island of Ireland. People have said that BIPA is just a talking shop, but in my view, it has a meaningful role. Apart from anything else, given the history of British and Irish relations, it can't be a bad thing to be on first name terms with so many Irish politicians, along with those from the other jurisdictions.

Sometime after I left Northern Ireland, I was invited to a fundraising event that the SDLP was holding in a West End hotel. I was pleased to see John Hume, the Irish nationalist politician who was awarded a Nobel Peace Prize in 1998. I had got to know him quite well over the years, and always had an enormous amount of respect for him. His critics said that he had been so passionately concerned to further the peace process that he ignored the needs of his own party. But I felt that his dedication was both admirable and essential to the cause of peace. He not only played a major part in getting the peace process underway, he was key to getting Gerry Adams involved. When Mary Robinson's time as president of Ireland came to an end in September 1997, John was believed to be in a good position to try to become her successor. However, he felt that he had to concentrate on supporting the peace process rather than being a senior figure in Dublin.

Sadly, in later years, John developed dementia. At the fundraiser, I was very sad to see how this had affected such a great political figure. At one point, John saw me and came over to ask: 'Who are these people? I don't think I know them.' I reminded him who some of the event's attendees were and he seemed to recover a bit. Later, he was asked to sing 'Danny Boy', which he did brilliantly. There wasn't a dry eye in the house. Certainly not mine.

Part Five

CAMPAIGNER

I.

The attacks on the World Trade Center in New York on 11 September 2001 changed so much in global politics. We are still feeling the effects of that seismic event now. For the Labour government, it marked a great shift from a focus on domestic policy to international relations, as we all became familiar with the term 'war on terror'.

There was criticism from some quarters over the decision to send British troops into Afghanistan in 2001. But at least we knew exactly who was responsible for the attacks on New York and where they were. However, I was horrified by the moves towards the invasion of Iraq in late 2002 and early 2003, and felt it was largely about forcing regime change, not national security for the US or the UK, as we were told. It was a very shocking and turbulent time. I was the chair of the Labour peers, and every ten days or so, the US Embassy would phone to ask me what the views of the Labour Party were regarding a possible military intervention. I responded that I felt that there was strong opposition to any British involvement and reported these exchanges to the meetings of Labour peers, who seemed to be largely in agreement.

We had a few debates in the Lords on the situation in Iraq before the intervention but there was never a vote. Ever since then, I have kicked myself for a major political failure on my part. Why on earth didn't I move an amendment that took note of the situation in Iraq and added the words 'but declines to support military action unless endorsed by the Security Council of the United Nations'? Perhaps I was influenced by the fact that I had been a minister a short time previously and felt I ought to be careful about launching an attack on the government of which I had been a member. Perhaps I simply didn't think of it. Admittedly, anyone else in the Lords could have moved such an amendment, but I have never forgiven myself for failing to take the initiative. It would not have been passed, so would have had no bearing on the outcome, but it would have helped some of my colleagues to take a public stand. I was very angry at myself that I had not used this lever available to me to at least do something.

My friend and parliamentary colleague Robin Cook MP was the former Foreign Secretary, and now Leader of the House of Commons. I had always had a very high opinion of Robin, both as regards his political effectiveness and his views. He invited me to be his Labour contact in the Lords as part of a small group that he consulted regularly. It was clear from our discussions, which also involved some back-bench MPs, that he was deeply unhappy about the preparations for intervention and that he would almost certainly have to resign should the government proceed.

I was in the public gallery on 17 March, the day of the critical Commons debate on whether to go ahead and join the Americans in taking military action in Iraq without UN Security Council backing or support from most of our European neighbours. In one of the most dramatic parliamentary occasions in recent years, Robin Cook made his resignation speech, stating that he intended to vote against the government the next day. It was a brilliant denunciation of government policy, which seemed to command a lot of support on the Labour benches. I noticed that sitting near me in the public galleries was Lord Philip Hunt, a health minister. I was not surprised when he also announced his resignation from the government the following morning.

The vote to approve military action in Iraq went through by 412 votes to 149, with 83 Labour MPs rebelling against the government. British troops entered the country with their American partners two days later. I believe that the distraction of Iraq took away our focus from Afghanistan and what we were trying to do there, with very serious long-term consequences.

In 2009, I discovered that Baroness Ann Taylor, a defence minister, thought it would be useful for some of us to visit Afghanistan. A group of politicians from both Houses was to travel to Helmand Province to get a first-hand understanding of what it was like for the troops working out there. I was very keen to do this, so I put up my hand, and was selected.

Before we left, we received a number of briefings at the Ministry of Defence, including on the overall situation in Afghanistan, the politics and the threats from the Taliban. One briefing covered what to do if we were taken hostage. This was very illuminating about what to do in such a situation and the risks involved.

We flew out from RAF Brize Norton. In some ways, this is like a civilian airport, with members of the armed forces and their families flying to Cyprus, the Falkland Islands and Germany. However, it was clear who was going to Afghanistan as all the troops wore combat gear. We were issued with helmets and flak jackets. The planes were painted in black camouflage because we could only take off and land at night.

The plane was carrying a lot of electronic gear, so there was limited seating. The troops on board were savvy and had brought their sleeping bags with them, whereas ours were stowed away with our baggage. So, the soldiers found bits of floor to sleep on, whereas we had to spend the night sitting up. There was a refuelling stopover at a NATO base somewhere in Turkey. As we approached Afghanistan, we were ordered to put on our flak jackets and helmets before we landed in Kandahar. At the airbase, we waited for another plane to take us on to Camp Bastion. It was bringing two soldiers to Kandahar who had been injured by IEDs (improvised explosive devices). In the meantime, our plane from Brize Norton was being converted into a 'medevac' – a flying ambulance – with teams of nurses and doctors, ready to fly the injured men to a hospital in Selly Oak, Birmingham, which was specially geared to military casualties.

Camp Bastion, in Helmand Province, was then exclusively a British base – companies of US Marines would move in soon after our visit to their own neighbouring camp. We spent the next day and a half meeting the camp commandant and many of the troops and other staff. We went out of the camp to watch the Afghan army being trained. I asked the commandant whether visitors got in the way of serious operations. He said that the troops all welcomed the interest that was shown and hoped that we would have a better understanding of their work at Camp Bastion. Morale among the troops seemed very high, even though they frequently had to leave the camp to go on dangerous missions from which some might not return. The food was very good, and the troops could watch football matches and films on TV more easily than back at home. But we were warned not to switch on our mobile phones as the Taliban were sophisticated enough to pinpoint a phone and attack it with a rocket.

The medical facilities at Camp Bastion struck me as being excellent. While we were there, two Afghans were flown in by helicopter as medical emergencies. They were quickly stretchered from their planes to the operating theatre where teams of doctors and nurses were waiting.

There was a large motor vehicle repair facility, which looked a bit like a car factory. We were shown the different designs of vehicles with their armour plating and other protective devices. We were told that it was always a challenge to design safety measures for the vehicles in anticipation of the deadly weapons that might be used against them.

We then flew back to Kandahar, a base that had troops from many countries. That night, we stayed in small barrack rooms, eight of us on bunks. I was in one of the top ones, to which I climbed somewhat unsteadily via a little table on which the man below had put his glasses, water, etc. In the middle of the night, the alarm sounded and the loudspeakers shouted, 'Rocket attack, rocket attack!' We had been told that if that were to happen, we had to lie on the floor and put on our flak jackets and helmets. My problem was that it was pitch dark and I could not see how to climb down from the top bunk. I quickly decided that the risk of having a bad fall exceeded the danger of rockets, announced that I was staying in bed and pulled the sleeping bag over my head. My roommates all did likewise, although one person did put his flak jacket on. By the time the all-clear sounded, I was asleep.

On the morning of 7 July 2005, London suffered terrorist attacks that killed fifty-two people and grievously injured and traumatised many hundreds. While the responders worked to pick up the pieces and Londoners tried to go back to normal life, there was pressure on the government for a clear response to this atrocity, alongside stories in the media that the security services had not done enough to identify the threat posed by the young attackers.

The government introduced a new terrorism bill to the Commons in October that year. A number of concerns about civil liberties were raised, and most strongly around the proposal to allow terrorism suspects to be detained for ninety days without charge. Many of us felt that – even in the face of threats that the UK was exposed to – to allow someone to be kept prisoner for three months before the police or security services were forced to either let them go or charge them was in direct opposition to basic human rights and not justifiable. A number of Labour MPs rebelled and the motion was defeated.

There was a further attempt to increase the limit to forty-two days in 2008, which caused a lot of anxiety, particularly to Labour MPs. Eventually it just scraped through the Commons, but only with DUP support. I had recently managed to get myself appointed to the Joint Committee on Human Rights, which comprises six members of the Commons and six from the Lords. We had been very critical of the proposed forty-two-day period and I had no intention of voting for it when the bill reached the Lords.

Not even those with experience of working within the security services were in favour of the extension. Baroness Manningham-Buller, the former head of MI5, had used her maiden speech in July 2008 to address the issue. She said that traditionally maiden speeches are short and uncontroversial, adding: 'I can do short.' She argued that there was a vital balance to be struck between civil liberties and national security, and called the proposal unworkable 'on a practical basis or on a principled one'. In six minutes, she totally demolished the case for forty-two days.

As the day of the Lords vote approached, I was asked three times by our leader in the House whether I would support the government, to which I said no. The whips asked me several times, and again I said no. Then the whips asked me if I would like to take the day off, to which I said no. Finally, Gordon Brown, then prime minister, called me directly. The country was deep into the financial crisis at this point; the bailout of the banks happened in the same month. We had an eight-minute telephone conversation in which Gordon made the argument that he did not want the Labour Party to look divided. Under my breath, I muttered that the best way to keep a united party was to pull the clause. I merely said to Gordon that I was very sorry, but I was totally committed. I would be willing to do virtually everything that he asked me to do, but not on this issue. He finished by saying that I was a good friend.

I warned the Lords minister in charge of the bill that the government would lose, which is what happened. No attempt was made to reverse our decision in the Commons. I think this was mainly because Labour MPs had seen what had happened in the Lords and realised that only the DUP had saved the government last time in the Commons. So that was the end of it. The government's arguments had been that so much terrorist crime was international and the evidence was often based on electronic material, so it would take longer to bring it together. However, there was little evidence to this effect, and it was therefore not surprising that the measure failed to pass its parliamentary test.

I found the Joint Committee on Human Rights to be the most interesting of all the select committees on which I served. I was used to scrutinising legislation of course, but looking at bills in order to identify where they may contravene human rights standards – such as those set out in the European Convention on Human Rights – was very engaging work. As with all select committees, the members had a lot of freedom to choose the areas we wished to investigate.

As a member of the JCHR, I visited Yarl's Wood in Bedfordshire, an immigration and detention centre where foreign nationals without the correct paperwork allowing them to be in the UK are held, sometimes before being removed from the country. People were often picked up in dawn swoops and taken there. The centre was regularly in the news in the 2000s due to protests by inmates and accusations of mistreatment by staff.

It was a depressing experience to see so many people locked up. I talked to a mother and three of her children who had been living in the Birmingham area. The immigration authorities and police had arrived very early in the morning, before the children went to school and college. One of the boys was a passionately keen cricketer, who had already had a trial for

Warwickshire. In the swoop, the family did not have time to get much together by way of their belongings and the young man had lost all his valuable cricket gear. He said to me, 'They picked on us, when we are all in education, and playing sports, and left untouched by the drug dealers in our neighbourhood.' I was happy to be part of a campaign, which included John Bercow MP (before he became the Speaker of the House of Commons) and Dr Evan Harris MP, in which we argued that children should not be kept in detention.

II.

When I arrived at Liverpool Street Station on a train from Prague in 1939, I was lucky in so many ways. My father was waiting for me and he could provide a roof over my head. My mother was later able to join us. While many of the other children on my train did not have family waiting for them, foster parents had been arranged. They had somewhere to go; adults looking after them. We entered a society that welcomed and supported us; we were able to enrol in a school to learn English. That is not the experience of so many child refugees today.

Children fleeing war face much greater hardship than I did back in 1939. Although the journey from Prague to London had seemed interminably long, there is no comparison with the journeys being undertaken by thousands of children even as I write. For many of them, the journey can take years and is fraught with danger, uncertainty and the threat of abduction, or worse.

Early in 2016, Save the Children carried out a survey of unaccompanied child refugees in various parts of Europe. The previous year, we had begun to use the term 'refugee crisis' to reflect the huge number of people arriving in Europe and the difficulties that the countries they reached first faced when dealing with such numbers. The UN estimated that about three-quarters came from Syria, where peaceful anti-government protests had turned into civil war; Afghanistan, following the withdrawal of many NATO troops and an increase in violence; and Iraq, where ISIS/ISIL was increasingly taking control and causing people to fear for their lives.

Save the Children's first estimate suggested that there were 26,000 unaccompanied child refugees. Following further work, they revised this figure, estimating that the real number of unaccompanied child refugees currently somewhere in Europe was nearer to 95,000. Equally alarming were Interpol figures that recorded some 10,000 people as having arrived and then gone missing. It's a frightful thought that young children can disappear like this in Europe and be exposed to the danger of exploitation. Save the Children said that it would be appropriate for Britain to take its fair share of these children, about 3,000.

In September 2015, a new immigration bill had been introduced to the Commons. This was the same month that the body of Alan Kurdi, a two-year-old Syrian boy was photographed washed up on a Mediterranean beach after the boat in which his family had been trying to reach the Greek island of Kos had capsized. The image went around the world and became a symbol of the tragic human cost of war and the plight of refugees trying to escape it. Yvette Cooper MP, at the time the chair of the Commons Select Committee on Home Affairs, approached me to discuss putting down an amendment in the committee stage of the bill in the Lords. The aim was to force the government to take some responsibility for helping children who arrived in Europe alone and without family connections, rather than leaving the crisis for other European countries to deal with.

I had been in close contact with the wonderful organisation Safe Passage, who I continue to liaise with now. Their work includes helping refugees with the incredibly complex legal procedures involved in reuniting families who have escaped war zones, and campaigning for safe and legal routes for those needing to seek asylum in Europe. I was very pleased to have their expert input and, after some discussion, I put down an amendment using the following wording:

Unaccompanied refugee children

(1) The Secretary of State must, as soon as possible, make arrangements to relocate 3,000 unaccompanied refugee children who are in European countries to the United Kingdom.

(2) The relocation of children under subsection (1) shall be in addition to the resettlement of children under the Vulnerable Persons Relocation Scheme.

The second point was intended to make sure that the government couldn't argue that they were doing this already under another scheme launched in 2014, mainly aimed at helping Syrians fleeing civil war.

Even before my amendment came up for debate, I sensed there was some concern on the government side. I had several conversations with Lord (Michael) Bates, the government minister responsible for the latest immigration bill in the Lords. I always felt that Michael was not only a decent minister but a good man, and in my conversations with him I had an inkling that his heart was not in the government's position, though he did his best to oppose my amendment. The following spring, Michael announced his resignation as minister so that he could undertake a sponsored trek across South America for charity.

I was then asked to see the Home Secretary, Theresa May, who had been appointed to the role as part of the formation of the new Conservative government in 2010. I knew her a little having met her at one of Nicky Winton's birthday parties, as she was the MP for Maidenhead, where he lived. I thought it was slightly unusual for a senior minister to see a back-bencher in the Lords, but I was delighted to meet her on the afternoon of Budget Day. We had a very agreeable talk, but her aim was to persuade me that I should not move an amendment stipulating child refugees from Europe.

The reason was that prime minister David Cameron had made it clear to other European leaders that Britain would not take refugees that were currently in camps in Europe because, he argued, it would have a magnet effect and encourage others to attempt to enter Europe, thereby increasing the number of refugees. He had received criticism earlier that year for referring, on ITV news, to a 'swarm' of people wanting to come to Britain. Sometimes also called a 'pull factor', this was a line often taken by the Tories at the time that ignored or diminished the reasons why people were leaving their homes and undertaking dangerous, gruelling and uncertain journeys across Europe. I replied that the 'magnet effect' was unproven, whereas the thousands of unaccompanied child refugees in Europe was a harsh fact. These were very vulnerable young persons in danger of being lured into prostitution, criminality or being trafficked in some way.

Theresa May made the specific suggestion that if I were to withdraw the amendment, she would add 3,000 people to the Syrian Vulnerable Persons Relocation Scheme and most of these would be children. It was a 'bribe' offered to keep me quiet. I pointed out that I was totally committed to the amendment and could not withdraw it. I said we could do both – my amendment and 3,000 extra displaced Syrians, which Theresa May could not accept. I had a sense that the drive to oppose my amendment was coming from the prime minister rather than the Home Secretary, and slightly suspected that she was more sympathetic to my amendment than she was able to admit, though of course I cannot prove it. We ended the conversation on friendly terms.

In the event, the 3,000 additional numbers that Theresa May had offered me stayed in the system, much to the surprise of many NGOs, who could not understand where the new total of 23,000 had come from. I didn't know whether it was simply a cock-up by the Home Office or a humanitarian gesture. In any case, I decided it was sensible to keep very quiet about it in case, once alerted to it, the Home Office withdrew the offer.

On 9 February 2016, my amendment was debated. It passed in the Lords with a majority of 80 – 300 votes to 220. As it made its way to the Commons, we began putting pressure on as many Conservative MPs as possible to receive their support. Yvette Cooper MP and her team played a large part in this. We sent emails to any MPs who we thought might be sympathetic and held a briefing for MPs of all parties to make the case for the amendment. There was a clear and pressing problem that the government had the power to address. I felt that the numbers involved made it quite a modest proposal – 3,000 children worked out to an average of just seven per local authority, Safe Passage had calculated.

In the meantime, I was in close contact with several of the NGOs who were working with refugees, especially in the 'Jungle' in Calais. The origins of the Jungle were in the Sangatte Red Cross camp that opened in 1999 to house those who had come from Kosovo, Iraq and Afghanistan. By early 2016, it had been closed, demolished and sprung back up again a number of times. My first visit was as part of a delegation of

NGOs, campaigners and five rabbis. I was told that the camp had been relocated some distance from its earlier location, and that the French government and the local authority had used tear gas and rubber bullets to move the refugees. I asked the NGOs how this could possibly be justified or necessary. I was told that the region near Calais had a strong Front National presence and the authorities wanted to demonstrate how tough they could be. But I don't believe the government could oppose fascism effectively by adopting the methods of fascism.

My reaction to the Jungle was that it was both utterly depressing and yet exhilarating. Depressing because of the terrible conditions in which people were living; exhilarating because the refugees' reaction to this showed the triumph of the human spirit. The camp had a café, where we had a meal. There was a small row of shops and a school, a church and, I believe, a mosque. We saw NGOs doing wonderful work there, including Safe Passage, Help Refugees and Care4Calais. They introduced me to nine Afghan boys and gave me documentation about each of them. On my return, I sent this to the Home Office as another way to ensure these children were properly identified and in the system. Ironically, within a week, four of the boys had made it to Britain having climbed onto lorries. This, of course, was a highly dangerous thing to do, and one boy had been killed a few weeks before my visit doing just that.

We were all very affected by what we saw. It was a lot to take in. We were having a debrief at Calais station before returning on the Eurostar. Commenting on something to do with British government policy, one of the rabbis said, 'That's a load of crap.' Before adding, 'I should explain that "crap" is a rabbinical term.'

On 25 April, the amendment – which had by now been termed 'the Dubs Amendment', rather to my surprise – was debated in the Commons. This was a media description and not terminology I would have initiated. There had been increasing media interest. I did countless interviews, both for British radio and television and for some broadcasters abroad, in America and on the Continent. The fact that I had come to Britain as an unaccompanied child refugee made the whole issue more interesting to the media. I was sometimes asked whether I was driven solely by my childhood experiences, but had to insist that the amendment had its own humanitarian logic. Of course, my background gave me an additional emotional involvement.

There are small galleries for members of the Lords in the lower house; during the debate I sat above the Labour benches so that I could eyeball the Tories. I was alone in that gallery, so I was obvious. One or two of the Tories waved at me and John Bercow MP, the Speaker, nodded. The best speech from the Labour benches was made by Jo Cox MP, who was so tragically murdered just a few weeks later. Because I was sitting above her I couldn't see her as she spoke, but I heard the brilliant speech she made, drawing on her insights from her experience while working with Oxfam on behalf of refugees.

The division was called and I saw at least one Tory MP dithering when we had expected backing. The amendment, which had total support from the parliamentary Labour Party, the SNP, the Lib Dems and from a few Tories, was lost by 294 votes to 276. The government did not contribute to the debate or raise any objections other than to invoke financial privilege, for which they were criticised by the Speaker. This is a somewhat arcane parliamentary concept. Although all legislation must go through both Houses, only the Commons can deal with financial matters – taxation and spending. Virtually every amendment to a bill that comes from the Lords will have some cost to the public purse, so the clerks in the Commons certify through the Speaker that financial privilege is involved. It is normally waived by the government but if invoked, as in this case of the amendment on child refugees, this constitutional restriction stops the Commons from insisting on the amendment to the bill. The government in effect rejected the amendment without giving any other reason, thereby neatly avoiding having to defend its position that it should not help 3,000 unaccompanied children, who had left warzones and were now alone and unsafe in Europe, to come to Britain, at a time when the public was acutely aware of the crisis unfolding on the other side of the Channel.

I was very disappointed and felt that the government's approach had been shabby. After the vote, I went downstairs to chat with Yvette Cooper and others in the corridor behind the Speaker's chair. Home Secretary Theresa May walked by, and I said to her, 'Well, you won that, but we haven't finished yet.' She smiled and walked on.

I knew that there was no real way to challenge financial privilege, as it's a constitutional issue. So I thought we should try a reworded amendment to be debated when the bill returned from the Commons to the Lords:

> Unaccompanied refugee children: relocation and support
>
> (1) The Secretary of State must, as soon as possible after the passing of this Act, make arrangements to relocate to the United Kingdom and support a specified number of unaccompanied refugee children from other countries in Europe.
>
> (2) The number of children to be resettled under subsection (1) shall be determined by the Government in consultation with local authorities.
>
> (3) The relocation of children under subsection (1) shall be in addition to the resettlement of children under the Vulnerable Persons Relocation Scheme.

The theory was that by leaving out the figure of 3,000 child refugees, it made it more difficult to calculate the expenditure involved and harder for the government to invoke financial privilege again. The amendment passed the Lords by an even larger majority than the first time – 279 to 172. I believed this was the best way to ensure Britain would do something to help at least some children stranded alone in camps in mainland

Europe, but I would later regret that we had no number to which to hold the government to account.

In the meantime, there were suggestions of more support from Conservative MPs, but perhaps the most critical factor was public opinion. The death toll of people trying to reach Europe by boat had reached shocking levels, and even elements of the usually hostile right-wing media were reporting on the desperation of many refugees. Normally the word refugee or migrant attracts opprobrium, but most messages that I received were supportive and people stopped me in the street to offer encouragement.

Only a tiny handful of messages were negative. One anonymous letter said, 'These child refugees will come here and become terrorists like you.' My campaigning on behalf of refugees has, from time to time, attracted abuse and threats. I am fully aware that I get very little of this compared with women in public life. It does seem that there is a close connection between racism and misogyny. But it's not pleasant to be told 'a pity you survived the Holocaust' or that the Parsons Green bombing was my fault because the bomber came from abroad. There was one occasion when the threat was personal and partly directed at my family. The police took that seriously and the culprit was arrested. When the abuse comes on Twitter, or X as it is now, my political advisor Candida does make a complaint, but not always with success. There are clearly some sick people in society who take advantage of the anonymity offered by electronic media.

In a wider sense, I regret the abuse that has been directed at many MPs, a tendency that seems to have increased in recent years. It is difficult to have an effective democracy when it is viewed as acceptable to denigrate politicians and throw abuse at them. The majority of MPs are committed to public service, almost certainly earn less than they would outside Parliament, and suffer serious encroachments on their freedom and their families' lives. There may be a few bad apples among MPs, but the majority are entitled to a modicum of respect for their dedication to public life.

Before the bill returned to the Commons, Theresa May asked to see me again. By then, it was clear that the government could not defeat the amendment a second time and that public opinion would not favour it if they tried. So they conceded, and I had the pleasure of seeing my amendment on the order paper in Theresa May's name. Success!

I had a telephone conversation with James Brokenshire MP, the Home Office Immigration Minister. He assured me that the government would accept both the letter and the spirit of the amendment. The government would take unaccompanied child refugees from Greece, Italy and France, provided they had arrived in Europe by 20 March. This seemed fine to me, and I was told that discussions were being started with the French, Greek and Italian authorities. Government officials also began to talk to local authorities in Britain who would be responsible for finding and vetting suitable foster parents – something that they have to do for all children who are to be fostered.

I was thrilled with the outcome, but I also found the whole experience overwhelming. It took me some time before everything sank in. Certainly, there were people who had helped with our campaign who grasped the significance of what had happened before it sunk in for me. I couldn't believe that after so many weeks and months of effort there was a successful outcome and my amendment had passed. I had not been prepared for the interest in my personal story, but was happy to talk about it, particularly if it helped people understand that offering safety to children displaced by war has long been a part of Britain's history. When so much of the damaging rhetoric referred to refugees as a large amorphous group, I think anything that humanises the story, that highlights the very difficult experiences of refugees as individuals, is valuable. Later, I took great pleasure in meeting children who, because of the amendment, had come to the UK in circumstances that paralleled my own arrival in the UK as an unaccompanied child refugee some eighty years earlier.

III.

I was dismayed at the way in which David Cameron handled our relations with the European Union, and I thought the decision to have a referendum on our membership of the EU was unnecessary and potentially disastrous for Britain. It was really called to resolve the internal problems of the Conservative Party. Worse still, the vote itself was poorly thought out, as there was no threshold for turnout nor a need for, say, a two-thirds majority vote for a decision to leave the EU to be binding.

During the referendum campaign, I decided to concentrate on the constituency where I now live when I am in London: Hammersmith. Most of my time was spent on the White City estate. My impression was that the people least persuaded to vote Remain were what we traditionally call 'white working class'. The great majority of those preferring Leave used immigration as their main argument.

One woman I spoke to said she was going to vote Leave

because of immigration. I said that not long ago, I had had a small medical procedure in Charing Cross Hospital. Except for one English nurse, all the team were immigrants, mainly from other EU countries. I pointed out that without immigrants, the health service would hardly be able to continue. A large proportion of health service workers were immigrants and looked after us extremely well. Her response was: 'It's not the ones who are here that I am worried about. It's the ones who will come here in the future.' It was about this time that prime minister Boris Johnson said that 75 million Turks (almost the country's entire population) were poised to enter Britain. It was a complete fabrication that was obviously intended to cause alarm and concern. Clearly there was no prospect of Turkey joining the EU at all, or certainly not for many years. At about the same time, Nigel Farage's UKIP had a nasty poster showing thousands of people ready to enter the UK. These lies, when added to the fabrications of extra money for the NHS, represented a toxic mixture of points against membership of the EU. I can't help thinking that Boris Johnson has a lot to answer for. Indeed, much of the Leave campaign was based on dishonesty and false claims.

As the polls closed on polling day, on 23 June 2016, I joined Steve Cowan, the Labour leader of Hammersmith and Fulham Council, for a drink in a pub opposite the town hall. By that time, I was feeling gloomier about the likely outcome than I ever had. We talked about refugees and the referendum, but when he invited me to attend the count, I declined because

I could not bear the thought of anti-EU results coming in from all over the country. Steve went into the town hall, and I went home to listen to the radio for most of the night in a state of increasing despair. That the result in Hammersmith, where I lived and had campaigned, was 70 per cent in favour of Remain, was of little consolation.

On the day after the referendum, I had agreed to speak at a rally on Wimbledon Common organised by the Merton Welcomes Refugees campaign, including two former Battersea Labour Party members, Peter Walker and Brenda Grant. My mood was gloomy, so it was a real effort to go. However, I cheered up at the commitment people showed in support of refugees. Whenever something terrible happens, it always brings out groups of people with a renewed determination to do something positive.

The outcome of the referendum led to an upsurge in hate crime. I know of people from European countries who have lived in the UK for decades who were told by their neighbours to 'get out'. There is a large Polish centre in Hammersmith and abusive comments were scrawled on the building after the referendum results. I was therefore pleased that Hammersmith and Fulham Council organised a march in July 2016 from Shepherd's Bush to Ravenscourt Park on the theme 'Love, not hate'.

As we have all come to realise, there were many consequences of leaving the EU that had not been thought through. One of the biggest concerns was the effect that the Leave vote would have on Ireland, North and South. Indeed, I had argued that if there was no other reason to vote Remain than Ireland itself, it would justify staying in the EU. I believe that the Good Friday Agreement would have been much harder to achieve, if at all, had both parts of Ireland not been within the European Union. EU support was an important factor in the peace process and in maintaining collaboration between the two communities in the North. When I considered the violence of the Troubles, and the enormous efforts made by many to establish a basis for peace in the run-up to and after the signing of the Good Friday Agreement, the thought of this being undermined by the referendum was frightening.

Many people now do not remember the days of the visible border between Northern Ireland and the Republic. At the height of the Troubles, it was studded with police and military checkpoints at the various crossing points, which were often targets for terrorists and could provide an uncomfortable experience for those wanting to cross. By 2016, the border had become completely invisible, and the Northern and Southern economies were becoming more and more integrated. One way of knowing in which jurisdiction one was driving was that the road signs were in either kilometres per hour or miles per hour. Where there used to be thirty places where one could cross the border, there are now around 300 roads on which one can freely move from North to South or vice versa. Those who remember the days of police and army checkpoints were alarmed at the prospect of a possible return to a hard border.

Already, the economy of the South had suffered a blow when the pound fell significantly against the Euro, thus cutting into the earnings of Southern producers selling to the North. Many of us were worried that the large volume of trade between Britain and Ireland would be jeopardised without a sensible agreement with Brussels. From evidence presented to the select committee on which I serve, it was clear that the tariff barriers between the UK and all of Europe would damage our industry, not only by increasing prices but also by imposing a great deal of bureaucracy that our membership of the EU obviated. It was worrying that some British government ministers seemed to believe that World Trade Organisation rules would be enough, rather than a Brexit agreement.

During the passage of the 'Brexit Bill', the Lords passed two amendments against the government. The first was to protect the position of EU citizens currently living in Britain, and the second was to ensure that Parliament would have a say when the negotiations finished and before the proposals went to the European Parliament. It was extraordinary to hear David Davis MP say that the government would have to consider whether the Lords should be abolished, given that we had voted to give the UK Parliament a say in negotiations. He claimed it somehow represented a rejection of the referendum result. The referendum did not stipulate what arrangement there should be with the EU after our departure. Given that the Leave campaigners argued they wanted to give the UK Parliament a greater say in our future than was possible as EU members, it was astonishing to hear from the same people that Parliament should have no involvement in the terms of our departure.

Traditionally, the European select committee in the Lords and the six sub-committees were regarded throughout the EU as the most thorough scrutiny process of any Parliament. After the Brexit referendum, everything changed. My sub-committee had intended to study relations between the EU and Turkey, but everything stopped. All the sub-committees had to turn their scrutiny to Brexit issues; mine looked at customs unions and the World Trade Organisation. There were months of gridlock in Parliament as Brexit was debated.

It soon appeared that the ministers responsible for negotiating the terms for our departure from the EU were not in control of their brief and had no clear position. No preparation, it seemed, had been undertaken in anticipation of a Leave outcome. Which of course had wide-ranging and significant consequences for trade and the economy, and far beyond. A witness from the motor industry pointed out that many components were imported from the continent (particularly Germany) and assembled into British cars, many of which were then sold back to other EU countries. Equally, he said that Britain manufactured more motor engines than we did cars, so many of these inevitably were exported to other parts of the EU. Two lots of tariff barriers with all the associated paperwork could be enough to move a lot of car production from Britain onto the continent of Europe.

What I found particularly worrying was the fact that post-Brexit, we would no longer be covered by the Dublin Regulation (sometimes called Dublin III), which sets out how asylum claims must be processed, including emphasising the importance of allowing families who have been separated to reunite, irrespective of where the latest family member to arrive in Europe wishing to seek asylum crossed the border. There are many reasons why families are separated when leaving their home country, and this principle had worked in making sure there was legal provision for an asylum-seeking child in one EU country to be able to apply to join relatives in another EU country. However, without it, many young people travelling unaccompanied, who did have family members already settled somewhere who wished to take them in and provide for them, would be left stranded without a legal claim. Accordingly, I put forward an amendment to the 2017 Immigration Bill that Britain should negotiate to continue the provisions of the Dublin Regulation, even after we had left the EU.

Meanwhile, the Home Office had been moving slowly in getting children to Britain from Calais under the terms of the Immigration Act amendment, despite all the positive noises I'd heard from James Brokenshire, the Home Office Immigration Minister. I was contacted by local groups in Britain that had been set up to help and support refugees. Some local authorities had very positive policies, both for child refugees and for families in the vulnerable persons scheme, but other councils were not helping. So, I spent time speaking to local meetings and, on occasion, talking to council leaders. Among the messages that I received were some from people who were willing to become foster parents or from organisations who were confident that they could find people who would foster child refugees. I even had a message from a Tory peer who said that his family were willing to foster. I contacted an appropriate NGO regarding those offers.

The number of children who had actually arrived in the UK either under the terms of the amendment or to reunite with family members, as per the Dublin Regulation, which would stay in effect until we formally left the EU, was low. This was concerning, and not helped by poor cooperation between the UK and French authorities. In the initial stages, British authorities were not allowed to identify children in the Jungle who would qualify under either criterion. At one point, we were told that the main effort was being made by just two volunteers from the organisation France Terre d'Asile, who were wandering around the camp with clipboards. That seemed a feeble approach, and I believed we ought to be trying much harder. When I pressed this in my meetings with government ministers, I was told that we did not want to fall out with the French in public, but apparently, harsh words were said behind the scenes.

Not long after Theresa May became prime minister and appointed Amber Rudd as Home Secretary, there was a reception in Parliament arranged by UNHCR and UNICEF during which Amber made a good speech and talked about vulnerable children, to the point where I had high hopes that she would continue with the scheme for some time. I had not met her before and introduced myself saying, 'I'm the person who has been causing you a lot of trouble.' To which she replied with some emphasis, 'Yes, you have!'

I was now receiving many invitations to speak at meetings on behalf of refugees. It was impossible to accept them all. I always felt guilty on the occasions that I had to say no. Once, I was asked to speak at Friends Meeting House in London, as part of a large anti-racism and pro-refugee rally. I spoke to a workshop of several hundred people and then in the plenary. Jeremy Corbyn, who had by then been elected leader of the Labour Party, and Diane Abbott arrived to a standing ovation. Jeremy began to make his speech and the organisers urged me to go on the platform with them. Eventually I joined them; Jeremy put his arms round me, full of praise for my efforts. The following Monday at the meeting of the Parliamentary Labour Party, Jeremy was questioned as to why he had been to a Socialist Workers Party event. He replied that it was all right because Diane Abbott was there and that Alf Dubs also spoke. While the SWP have been active in campaigning on behalf of refugees and I welcome their commitment, I have felt that I should not become too associated with them as I do not share their politics.

In 2016, Ishmael, a Syrian boy, came to the Lords for work experience. He had been the first to arrive under the amendment that I had introduced to the 2016 Act. On several occasions, we did joint meetings at schools about the rights of refugees. I found that school students were invariably a receptive audience. Perhaps because young people tend to have such an innate sense of fairness, which adults can sadly lose. On one occasion, I was invited to speak at a maintained school in Tower Hamlets, as the boys – most of whom were Muslim – were working on a project about the Kindertransport and the Holocaust. When we reached the Q&A, the first question was: 'What do I say to anyone who denies the Holocaust ever happened?' I thought it was a brilliant question and a sign of the students being very aware.

I was also often asked to speak to faith groups, especially by the Jewish community. I made it clear that I am a humanist, but they didn't seem to mind. Indeed, a rabbi once said to me, 'Half the congregation don't believe in God either, but they come here for a sense of community.' On one occasion, I was speaking at a traditional synagogue and was disconcerted that the women were sitting at the back for the service, though they came forward when I spoke. I went on to speak in Trafalgar Square at an Iftar, the meal eaten by Muslims at sunset to break their fast during Ramadan. I made virtually the same speech to both audiences.

The open Iftar in Trafalgar Square turned out to be a wonderful occasion. It was great to see around 2,000 people sitting there waiting for sundown. It was notable that there were hundreds of women present, in contrast to some Muslim events where older men tended to be in the majority. Afterwards, I spoke with a French woman who gestured at the people sitting there. She said this couldn't happen in France as there was too much Islamophobia there, and that was why she had moved to the UK. I wonder if the contrast would still apply after the 7 October Hamas attacks in Israel and the Israeli attacks in Gaza.

Public attention was kept on the issue of unaccompanied child refugees by people working hard in a number of quarters. I paid another visit to Calais in September 2016 along with several NGOs and the actors Vanessa Redgrave and Joely Richardson, Vanessa's daughter. I had previously been introduced to Vanessa by Maurice Wren, a chief executive of the Refugee Council. Vanessa clearly wanted to be involved in campaigning and threw herself into this with total commitment. She took a full part in all our meetings and discussions, and insisted on walking around the Jungle rather than travelling in the vehicle that was provided. Subsequently, she made a documentary about refugees in Europe called *Sea Sorrow* – a very moving film that leaves me feeling quite shaken after every viewing. Vanessa is an incredibly effective and committed campaigner. It has been a privilege to cooperate with her.

One of the many demos to support refugees ended up with speeches in Parliament Square, including one by a young Syrian boy. Vanessa took part in this, as did her fellow actors Juliet Stevenson and Harriet Walter. I found it so impressive that many eminent people were willing to commit themselves to the cause of refugees.

Throughout my work on child refugees, I have met so many

young people who volunteered in the camps and elsewhere. They were in the most unselfish way possible giving up perhaps a year or more of their lives, jobs and income to help refugees and other vulnerable people. I found it a great privilege and honour to be able to work with them. It made me realise that Britain was not just full of money-grabbing bonus-seeking bankers, but that we had some utterly selfless, wonderful people. Perhaps I might single out Liz Clegg, a firefighter from Birmingham, who gave up her job to look after the mother and child centre in the Jungle. Some of her work was carried out from a London double-decker bus, parked in the camp. I think it had been bought by Juliet Stevenson for use there.

In January 2017, I was invited to Vanessa Redgrave's eightieth birthday party at the Royal Court Theatre in Sloane Square, London. Joely asked me if I would pay a tribute. The same afternoon I had been speaking at a Holocaust Memorial Day event, from which I had to hurry in a taxi. When I got there, the party had already begun and the actor Benedict Cumberbatch was on the platform, reading poetry. Many talented people either spoke from the platform or were connected by video from Hollywood and elsewhere. I became more nervous as time went on because each speaker was impressive beyond belief, and I thought my little contribution – a reading of 'Refugee Blues' by W. H. Auden – would appear pathetic by comparison. But what a privilege it was to be invited to such a fantastic occasion.

*

In late October 2016, the French authorities began clearing the Jungle and dispersing people to many parts of France. The exact number of people living there was unknown – estimates usually ranged from 7,000 to 9,000. There was concern that it would be very hard to keep track of the unaccompanied children once they were moved on and difficult to make sure their cases were advanced. At this point, the Home Office sent officials to locate unaccompanied children and assess their eligibility to come to the UK. We argued that it was important to get as many young people as possible to the UK in time for the next school term so that they did not lose another year of education.

Slowly, children began to arrive. The press was there in full force at the Home Office's Lunar House in Croydon and managed to photograph some of the Dublin Regulation arrivals. Some journalists maintained that they were older than eighteen and the media made much of the story. I pointed out that the world would not come to an end if a nineteen-year-old arrived in Britain rather than a seventeen-year-old, and that secondly, when a young person had travelled halfway across the world over many months, if not years, it might be that they would appear older than a child who had not endured this experience. However, the whole episode about age was not helpful, not least because so many of us had worked hard to get the public opinion on the side of Britain taking more child refugees.

The following month, the Home Office published new

eligibility criteria for unaccompanied child refugees. These said that we should take young children under ten; girls who the French authorities had said had been sexually abused; and children coming from Syria and Sudan. We protested this, especially as it meant excluding Afghans, Eritreans, Ethiopians and Somalis. All of these children were coming from countries that posed enormous threats to people's safety, including persecution and the risk of recruitment into armies and paramilitary groups. They too were alone and in danger. The Home Office put up the feeble defence that, statistically, Eritreans and Ethiopians had a slightly lower chance of achieving refugee status than did Syrians. This represented to my mind a clear breach of the 1951 Geneva Convention, which states that the determination of refugee status should be based upon individuals and not on a collective. You must not lump people together but assess their eligibility based on their individual circumstances. When I contacted UNHCR in London, they told me that they had protested strongly to the Home Office about this, but diplomatic protocol prevented them from showing me a copy of the letter they had sent.

It was very frustrating that things were moving so slowly, particularly when we knew that there were local authorities and foster families prepared and able to help these children, who remained at risk while the government prevaricated.

IV.

Largely because of its geographical location, Greece had been on the frontline of the refugee crisis. It still is, with huge numbers of people living in camps and facing great uncertainty, while the Greek government has to cope the best it can.

In early January 2017, I visited Greece with Help Refugees and Safe Passage. I was to have a discussion with officials and NGOs in Athens, then visit some of the camps north of Thessaloniki. Clearly the Greek government was in a very difficult financial situation, and had 65,000 refugees in the various camps on the islands and the mainland. We estimated that this included 10,000 children, of whom 2,500 were unaccompanied. I found the situation in the camps even more depressing and desperate than what I had seen in Calais. Those I visited were on industrial estates, sometimes in large warehouses and sometimes comprised of flimsy mobile homes. The temperature was bitterly cold, perhaps below zero. There was virtually no heating, as the electricity supply did not have capacity for heaters. Adjacent to one of the warehouses was a small wooden school that the refugees had dismantled for firewood. One of the camps had a food kitchen, and twice a day they drove into the centre of Thessaloniki to feed the eighty or so refugees sleeping in the streets.

When I asked who oversaw the camps, it seemed that nobody had overall responsibility. The Greek army had provided some of the infrastructure and for the rest it was up to NGOs like Help Refugees to help those living there to survive. There was one small glimmer of hope in a housing development, which Help Refugees had acquired to allow some refugees to have their own accommodation with their own front door. This was a drop in the ocean in relation to the problem but was interesting to see in action. The NGOs told me that the Greek Ministry for Education had said the children should go to a nearby primary school. Initially, there were protests at this from the Greek parents. Then when the Greek mothers saw that their own children were playing happily with the Syrian children, they became much more sympathetic and came to the block of flats asking how they could help.

The local Thessaloniki council had arranged a week of parties for local children. A Greek official, much to his credit, had arranged that children from the refugee camps could also take part. Each day, several coach loads of mothers and children went along. I joined them and saw the spectacle of this large hall, with dodgems, trampolines, ice skating and other funfair activities. The place was warm, and I shall never forget seeing mothers in hijabs and their sons and daughters driving round in dodgem cars. It was also delightful to see Syrian children trying to learn to skate on ice, which they were probably seeing for the first time. I helped Father Christmas give out presents for each child. A little girl of perhaps five was being shepherded back on the coach with her present under her arm when she broke away and rushed back to see Father Christmas again. One mother said it was the first really happy day she'd had for years. Then it was back to the bitter cold and bleakness of their day-to-day accommodation.

Shortly after my return from Greece, I went to Brussels as a member of the Organization for Security and Co-operation in Europe's (OSCE) parliamentary assembly, which is made up from representatives of fifty-seven countries and works to further democracy and human rights. In Brussels, our Migration Committee was addressed by one of the commissioners. After about half an hour, we asked if there would be questions. He said yes but went on talking and then said he had to leave.

Then we went to Geneva, where our first meeting was with the International Committee for the Red Cross. We asked them what they were doing to help the Greeks with their difficulties, and the answer was: 'That is not in our mandate.' When we asked who was responsible for the camps, we were told that it was up to the Greek government. It was a depressing comment given the difficulties facing that government.

While some NGOs, small organisations and individuals were working as hard as they could to provide people with the basic stuff of life and some respite from the stark difficulties of their situations – as I had seen at the party in Thessaloniki – it was clear that there was no overall strategy or policy at the highest level, even though this coordination was desperately needed. The international community was doing far too little to help with the refugee crisis.

Things continued to move slowly as regards unaccompanied children coming over from France, especially now that the Jungle had been cleared. I appreciated that government speaks with one voice, but I sometimes felt that some of the ministers, including Baroness Susan Williams, the Home Office minister in the Lords, were quite sympathetic to my arguments but could not say so. It was agreed that I should have regular meetings with Susan in the Lords to keep me updated on developments. This often it left me criticising the government, with Susan being unable to respond on any point of substance. In fairness, I got on well with her and it enabled me to have my say on what I was hearing from organisations I was connected with, like Safe Passage, who understood the situation better than most.

In February 2017, I was angry and disappointed when the government announced that the scheme covered by section 67 of the Immigration Act to identify and bring unaccompanied refugee children from Europe would finish by the end of

March 2017. At that point, only 200 children had come in under that category and the government said a further 150 would come in by the end March, at which point it would cease. When I thought of all the children I had seen struggling in camps in Calais and Greece, it was impossible to fathom how the government could think of stopping even the small measures it had committed to.

There was widespread outrage at this news. A number of newspapers ran stories on it and NGOs considered what they could do to challenge the decision. Yvette Cooper MP secured an urgent question in the Commons, and I was granted permission to ask a private notice question, which is the equivalent in the Lords.

The government put forward two reasons for bringing the scheme to an end. Firstly, they said that the existence of the scheme encouraged trafficking. This is quite illogical. Where there are safe routes out, trafficking does not get any customers. Where there are no safe routes out, then people become more desperate and will contemplate more risky means. Secondly, the government said that local authorities were no longer able to provide foster places for children, or independent supported accommodation for those aged seventeen or eighteen.

However, I talked to several council leaders who said that they were quite willing and able to provide more foster accommodation, and indirectly I heard from all over the country that local authorities had places that they could make available. I even asked a member of the Scottish Parliament for information about Scottish local authorities, with the result that I was asked to meet Angela Constance, then SNP Cabinet Secretary for Communities, Social Security and Equalities. She thought that Scottish local authorities were willing to step up, in particular Glasgow City Council. Councillor Steve Cowan, the Leader of the London Borough of Hammersmith and Fulham, said he was prepared to take more children and would encourage other councils to do the same. Steve was a brilliant supporter of the campaign. On one occasion, a member of his team of social workers took a day's holiday to go to Calais, see the situation for themselves and assess children as to their eligibility to come to the UK.

The NGOs and other people campaigning on behalf of child refugees were very keen to put as much pressure on the Home Office as we could so that the scheme would be restored. We reported all of our findings regarding the resources that were available in local authority areas for unaccompanied child refugees if the government would maintain the mechanism to allow them in. At Lib Dem and SNP conferences, resolutions were passed urging the government to take more unaccompanied child refugees. There was a strong sense that the Conservative government had moved against both parliamentary and public opinion. It is shameful that they used feeble excuses to make decisions that fly in the face of what so many people in Parliament and the general public believed to be right. It was this public opinion that I believe made the government concede to the amendment in the first place. I was as certain as ever that the wider opinion continued to be on the side of taking child refugees.

In the end, the overall total of refugee children permitted to resettle in the UK with foster families in the UK was 480. It was a far cry from the 3,000 I had been led to believe would be allowed. And a drop in the ocean when you consider the number of children that Save the Children had identified as being alone without their parents in various camps in Europe. I consoled myself with the fact that each of those 480 children was starting a new life in Britain. Though many would be suffering trauma as a result of their experiences – such as the boy I met who had seen his father killed in front of him in Damascus – and would require much care and support, they were much safer here and had the chance to build a life of stability. Plus, so long as we kept to the Dublin regulation after the withdrawal from the EU was complete, that gave provision for children to be reunited with family members here. However, I couldn't help but reflect that Britain had accepted around 10,000 unaccompanied child refugees who arrived by Kindertransport between the autumn of 1938 and September 1939 prior to the Second World War. We had the resources to do so much more.

I continued to look for ways that I could put pressure on the government. The best opportunities for this arose whenever a related bill was set to go through Parliament, as I could add an amendment that would trigger a debate. It was one way to bring about some concessions from the government that was set on making it harder and harder for refugees to come to this country legally.

When the Children and Social Work Bill was proceeding through Parliament, I proposed an amendment that pressed the government to ensure proper safeguarding and support of unaccompanied refugee children once they had arrived in the country. In March 2017, the Higher Education and Research Bill presented me with an opportunity to address an issue with access to higher education for people who had come here from war-torn countries but did not have full refugee status. In practice, this meant mainly Syrians who came to Britain under an immigration status called 'humanitarian protection'. This meant the same as refugee status with one important exception, namely that while those with refugee status could immediately apply for funding to have access to higher education, those with humanitarian protection had to wait for three years. This is clearly an anomaly and means that smart young people who had suffered greatly in many respects were missing out on completing their education.

The procedures for making amendments to bills are more relaxed in the Lords than in the Commons. It is straightforward to put down an amendment at committee stage. In the light of the minister's comments, one can then fine tune the amendment and have another go at report stage.

At very short notice, on the day of the Higher Education and Research Bill debate, I was asked to see Amber Rudd, the

Home Secretary, in her office in the Commons, where she was accompanied by Robert Goodwill MP, the Home Office minister, and some officials. Amber said that the government was sympathetic to eliminating the anomaly and that there had been discussions with UNHCR to grant all Syrians under the vulnerable persons scheme full refugee status, rather than merely humanitarian protection, which would entitle them to faster access to higher education. I felt this was a good move, although it might omit some people from countries other than Syria who get humanitarian protection and would not be covered by this measure. But as I was aware that there were very few of these, I told Amber Rudd that I was happy with it.

In 2019, I was devastated when the government dropped its commitment to negotiating the continuation of the Dublin Regulation EU arrangements after Brexit. This meant that child refugees would no longer have the right to join family members who were already settled in this country. This was a big blow with wide-reaching implications and would affect many people. It was also a surprise. I had moved an amendment to another Immigration Bill in 2017 that the UK should negotiate to keep the Dublin III provisions even after we had left the EU. This was eventually passed by both houses. Then to my dismay, the government deleted it from the Immigration Act 2019. I don't think I have ever been so angry.

I tried and failed to get it reinstated. Eventually, I was called for a meeting in the Lords to discuss this further.

I arrived in Baroness Williams' office to find that there were two other ministers present, including Brandon Lewis MP, the immigration minister, and seven officials, including one from the Cabinet Office. I thought that being outnumbered ten to one represented fair odds.

Brandon did most of the speaking and I was assured that the immigration rules provided an effective path for family reunion, without the need for the provision offered by the Dublin Regulation. When I expressed doubts about this, as the rules are Byzantine and open to interpretation in a way that legislation is not, Brandon asked me directly if I trusted him. Wishing to stay reasonably polite, I answered that even if I trusted him, I couldn't trust the government and that he might be moved to another post anyway. I now feel that was weak, and I wish I'd said, 'I don't trust any of you.' Indeed, not long afterwards, Brandon Lewis was appointed the Secretary of State for Northern Ireland. The flow of child refugees arriving from Europe for family reunion virtually dried up after we left the EU. So much for the assurances I was given.

The government continued to make it as difficult as possible for refugees to reach and claim asylum in the UK. It then took hostility to refugees one step further by making it illegal to arrive in the UK except by an authorised route. The problem is there are very few of these and none that covers the largest number of cases – Syrians, Afghans and people from the Horn of Africa. But of course, desperate people will always try. Such arrivals would, by the Act, be prevented from claiming asylum and presumably would be held in custody in the absence of any agreed return arrangements with EU countries. Indeed, practically the only country willing to accept people back is Albania. One result was that more and more people who had arrived – increasingly by the incredibly dangerous method of dinghies operated by people smugglers – became stuck in limbo.

When the Conservative government's Illegal Migration Bill came before the Lords in 2023, we passed twenty amendments against the government. I had an amendment to enable children who reached the UK even by means that were not approved by the Home Secretary to be able to claim asylum in the usual manner. The argument of the Labour front bench had been that we should support those amendments that had been moved by Tory or crossbench peers, as they would be most likely to attract Commons votes. In the event this didn't happen, and all but one of the twenty amendments were rejected by the Commons (only one on slavery was accepted by the government). I thought we would have done better to argue the real points of principle at stake than look for short-term tactical gains.

This Act inevitably increased the numbers that would need to be accommodated in hotels, at enormous cost to the taxpayer. There have been some 170,000 asylum seekers awaiting the outcome of their claims. Some wait for years and they are not allowed to work for all that time, thereby increasing the costs to the taxpayer even more. The expedient thought by the Home

Office to accommodate asylum seekers in disused army camps or in barges around the coast totally failed.

The so-called 'Rwanda Bill' was an attempt to remove some asylum seekers on a nine-hour flight to the African nation where the government would pay for them to be processed locally by the Rwandan authorities. This was at a time when the UK had accepted asylum seekers from Rwanda, while still claiming the country was safe. The government admitted that in practice only a small number of asylum seekers would be sent to Rwanda, but hoped that it would deter boat people from trying to reach Calais and then cross the Channel.

The whole idea was incredibly expensive – it cost some £400 million without ever taking effect – as well as surely being in breach of our obligations under the 1951 Geneva Convention on refugees. One of the first decisions by the newly elected Labour government in 2024 was to scrap the Rwanda scheme. The whole thing is a mess that will take a long time to sort out. Very little of the money spent in this area benefits anyone and does nothing to address the complicated issues that underpin the situation.

I have made several more visits to Calais. The last occasion was towards the end of 2023 when the *Daily Mirror* organised the day. This was the most depressing time that I ever experienced in Calais. The asylum seekers were sleeping in sodden fields, some in tents, others under tarpaulins. The Sudanese told me they had no money to pay traffickers, so depended on being asked to steer the boat or dinghy in return for a passage. Apart from the danger involved, this of course ran the risk that the UK authorities would charge them with being traffickers if they were caught, thereby attracting a more severe penalty. The asylum seekers were in bad shape and we had a whip round to buy footwear for some of them.

According to the NGOs we met, there was hardly enough food, perhaps one vehicle load a day. I saw people queuing for food when a truck arrived. The four representatives from the NGOs we met struck me as being under severe pressure. They also explained that if the asylum seekers were fingerprinted on arriving in Greece or in Italy, they would not be able to claim asylum in France. So much for the persistent view of Tory ministers that they could all claim asylum in France. The NGOs said there was a way round this, but it would require the services of expensive lawyers – almost certainly beyond the reach of these asylum seekers. They suggested that it would be helpful if the asylum seekers had access to social workers, who might be better placed to advise what was in each individual's best interests – lack of correct information and support being a major problem. Some of the asylum seekers did have family in the UK. But for most, the only connection appeared to be the English language, even if they hardly spoke it.

We encountered one Syrian family who suffered a genetic condition called Bloom Syndrome. Their daughter had died of this and the younger of their two sons was suffering from the same condition, while the mother was pregnant with their fourth child. The father had identified a doctor in Manchester who was a leader in the field. It seemed most improbable that the UK would let the family in, but time was of the essence given the mother's pregnancy. On our return, we spoke to the Manchester-based doctor who said he would treat the family if they were able to enter the country. In the meantime, he suggested two doctors in France who were also experts in this condition. With the support of *The Mirror*, we crowdfunded and raised a few thousand pounds to pay a doctor in France. Despite our efforts, the French doctors did not reply, and our subsequent attempts to contact the family failed. Later, we discovered that they had reached the UK by boat and were receiving treatment at a London hospital. The Home Office then wanted to move them to Scotland, against strong medical advice from the hospital that it would be risky to stop the treatment at that stage. I raised my concern at a meeting with a Home Office minister and asked that the family be allowed to stay in London. Their younger son died, but the family were allowed to stay in the southeast for medical reasons.

I have continued to raise the issue of reunion for child refugees, including when the Borders Bill reached the Lords in the autumn of 2025. Several NGOs, Safe Passage, the Refugee Council and others prepared an amendment which would largely reinstate the earlier Dublin III amendment.

The Labour whips asked me to withdraw this amendment, but I pointed out that it effectively represented Labour policy at the time of the 2017 and 2019 Acts and this amendment would show that we were clearly able to show a human rights-based approach, quite different from Reform policies.

In the event the amendment was soundly defeated as both the Tories and Labour whipped against it. But I will continue to fight for this issue, alongside others which may not be popular with the government, but upon which I hold strong beliefs. Among them is Shamima Begum, the young woman who was recruited as a minor from Tower Hamlets to join ISIS and whom the Tory government stripped of her British citizenship – a decision which I believe is wrong. It has been argued that Shamima has never publicly withdrawn her support for ISIS, but I would argue that, given she is living in a camp surrounded by ISIS supporters, it is unreasonable to expect her to risk her life in this way. As she was raised in the UK, I believe that she should return here, where she could both face justice and receive support.

In April 2026, I put down a motion questioning recent changes to immigration rules that would make it harder for refugees to successfully integrate; failed to restart the process for refugees to be reunited with their family members; and prevented some students from taking up educational opportunities in the UK. I had no intention of having a vote on this and made this clear to the whips. Nevertheless, the whips were unhappy that I had put it down at all. I argued that when a hundred Labour MPs had said the same thing, what was the problem with my getting it debated in the Lords? I am afraid the Chief Whip was not happy.

One of the pleasures of having reached this stage of my political career is that I have no political ambitions. I regard our leader Baroness Angela Smith and our Chief Whip Lord Roy Kennedy as friends. However, I have on occasion displeased the whips by raising issues that Labour supported in opposition, but no longer does in government.

I still have unfinished business which I continue to look for opportunities to raise, from returning the Parthenon Marbles to Greece, to reforming the House of Lords, rejoining the EU and introducing proportional representation and supporting human rights, especially for refugees and asylum seekers.

Ensuring we have a human rights-based approach for asylum seekers and refugees remains the issue closest to me. Because it is a lack of hope which so appals me about the plight of refugees today. Having visited camps in France, Greece and Jordan, I have found desperate people, including many lone children, who have no prospect of finding a new life. They may have survived the terrible experiences that led them to flee, but just surviving has become their lot. As we remember the terrible events of the Second World War and try to address the needs of refugees and asylum seekers today, it is my hope that we will also remember the humanity that was shown to children like me – and honour that humanity by standing together and once again welcoming those persecuted by war so they too can have hope for the future.

*

The question of retirement has never really arisen for me. After John Major left politics, he made some radio programmes about cricket, which I enjoyed very much. One day, I happened to see him, and I complimented him on those shows. He replied, 'Alf, there is a life outside politics; you should try it sometime!'

While I have been kept rather busy by life in politics, I have managed some outside interests. Our family has kept a home in the Lake District, which was our main base for several years. Ann and I both feel part of the community there. This gave us plenty of opportunity for fell walking, which had long been our passion. It puts things into perspective. At 1,000 feet up, the world's problems feel pretty small; at 2,000 feet up, the problems feel tiny; at 3,000 feet up, I think: what problems?!

Though I have found hill walking a highly therapeutic escape from political life, I have to admit I have not always kept the two entirely separate. I was part of a team that re-established an All-Party Parliamentary Group (APPG) on mountain rescue, acting as one of the officers with Rory Stewart MP as the chair. At that time, the Mountain Rescue Service in England had no public support at all, though in Scotland it had some government funding.

Apart from their day-to-day rescuing work on the Lake District fells, the local mountain rescue teams in Cockermouth were conspicuous for the fantastic rescue work they did during the 2009 and 2015 floods. In November 2009, the main street was six feet or more under water and virtually every shop was badly damaged. In Workington, one policeman died when he was swept away by flood water. The mountain rescue teams were the first on the scene and saved many people. It was sad to walk along the main street after the floods had subsided to see shops bare apart from humidifiers that were trying to get rid of the damp. Some of the shops were in very old cottages and it was a struggle to survive. It seems that such severe incidents, which used to happen perhaps once in a hundred years, have become a frequent occurrence and the government and local authorities will have to spend millions on precautionary measures. It is only the resilience and determination of many of the Cumbrians that the area manages to recover after each disaster.

The APPG of which I was a member wanted to make sure that the incredibly dedicated work by the mountain rescue teams was acknowledged. Most people do not seem to be aware that mountain rescue is a voluntary effort and that most of the teams raise the money themselves. Yet without mountain rescue teams, tourism in the Lake District and hill walking would be less safe for fell walkers and climbers.

The Cockermouth team came to London to receive an award, and I took them onto the terrace at Westminster. As a result of all this, I got to know them well. One day, they asked me if I would like to take part in a training day. I realised too late that what they wanted was a 'body' to bring down from the mountain. The team leader was Mike Park. We climbed up Grasmoor, to about two-thirds of the way from the top, and they then put me on a stretcher. I was totally immobilised as they were simulating a spinal injury. I wore a helmet and had protective visors. It was a strange experience, with eight members of the team sliding the stretcher down a steep scree slope. I was unable to move my head and could only see what was straight in front of me. Somebody asked afterwards if I had been scared, but I said that I felt safer than I would have done trying to scramble down such a steep slope.

I learned during the exercise what a high-tech mountain rescue operation is now. Altogether there were about eighteen people on the training day, and I was highly impressed by their professionalism and dedication. Fortunately, there are local employers who give them the necessary time off to go out and rescue people who become injured on the mountains. Of course, they also get some silly requests for help. One person phoned them from the edge of Crummock Water seeking help because he was late for dinner.

Every year there is an excellent book festival in Keswick in Cumbria, 'Words by the Water', whose president is Melvyn Bragg. There are always fascinating talks, and on one or two occasions I have been asked to chair the speakers. Once, my friend Chris Mullin spoke about his recently published diaries. He was asked whether the day of the political meeting was over. He thought not, but that book festivals had become the new forum for them. When he had been the MP for Sunderland it was a job to get eight people to attend a meeting, yet here were several hundred people paying £9 a head to listen to him.

The book festival in Keswick is always packed, a sign that there is a real hunger for literature of all kinds and insights provided by all sorts of authors.

In 2010, the Tory Government made renewed moves to privatise the Forestry Commission. We arranged a demo on top of the Whinlatter Pass to protest at this proposal, and several hundred people turned up. It was great to be on the fells in a forest demonstrating against the government. The government backed off because they realised there was such massive opposition to what they were trying to do.

However, I have managed to restrain myself from getting involved in village politics. There are debates about local planning and services reminiscent of plots on *The Archers*! I listen to the conversations but deliberately avoid entering; sometimes it is okay to remain a bystander. On 29 November 2022, I was awarded an honorary degree of Doctor of Laws by the University of St Andrews. I was delighted to accept.

One day in January 2023, a journalist contacted me. He said he was working on my obituary and asked if I could give him some information. I ignored the request. On the same day, I went to the parliamentary gym. They told me they had no record of my membership, although I was probably one of the longest-serving members. These two events occurring on the same day were rather disconcerting.

Then a few days later, I felt a bit odd as I got up at the end of a meeting of the Joint Commission of Human Rights. It all happened very suddenly. I took a cab home and felt terrible the following morning. I phoned my GP; we agreed that I couldn't get to the surgery so the doctor said she would come to my house at lunchtime. I was surprised but grateful that home calls were possible, given the pressure on GPs. Right on time, the doctor arrived. She carried out a few tests and called an ambulance to take me to A&E at Charing Cross Hospital. It took several MRI scans and one or two lumbar punctures to eliminate the possibility of a stroke. The eventual diagnosis was Guillain-Barré syndrome. It is a rare condition in which the immune system attacks the outlying nerves, affecting movement, senses, breathing and heart rate. I'd never heard of it, though I was later told that Tony Benn had it in the 1980s.

Within a day or so I was moved to intensive care. By this point, I could not walk nor swallow and could barely speak. I was 'nil by mouth' and had tubes coming in and out of various places, including oxygen. Intensive care is a weird experience. It is very noisy with lights flashing and alarms going off. Of course it was impossible to sleep. One night at about 3 a.m., a doctor came over to me and in my bewildered state I thought I heard her say, 'We know who you are!' I hope I replied, 'But don't tell anyone!' She turned out to be a consultant of German heritage and expressed an interest in the books I had on my table, not that I was capable of reading anything at that time. Apart from a political thriller, I had a book about the prime minister of Hungary, Viktor Orbán. We then had a conversation about Hungarian politics. It was all a bit surreal.

Candida visited me frequently while I was in hospital and I tried to do some work. It was not until some time later that I learned how ill I had been. I remarked to the nurses the irony that ten days earlier I had been playing tennis and hill walking. Now I couldn't even stand on my feet.

During my time in the ICU, I was given an infusion, the only drug that might help. After that, the only way to get better was through rehab. At some point I was helped to a bathroom and saw my face for the first time. I looked like a corpse and briefly wondered whether I should tell the doctors not to bother any more.

After nine days in the ICU, I was moved onto a normal neuro ward. One day a nurse brought in a therapy dog. It was delightful and sat on my bed for a few minutes. I can't remember how long it was before I was moved onto a rehab ward. As anyone who has had a prolonged stay in hospital knows, time moves very strangely there. At some point I got Covid and was quickly moved into isolation. This meant any visitors had to wear full protective gear.

In rehab, things slowly improved. I had a programme of classes and other activities. Some were clear, like a cookery class where I chopped garlic to help with my manual dexterity. The problem was the conversation class. By that time, my voice had recovered and I was enjoying being able to speak again, but the same could not be said of the other patients. I explained how it wasn't helping the other patients if I dominated the discussions and it was agreed I did not have to attend.

I got used to the hospital routine. It was always a pleasure when the night or day shift started work by introducing themselves to all the patients. I spent time walking round the floor where the rehab wards were located, first with help and then alone. Next, the rehab people felt I should try walking outside, which was more difficult because of the uneven roads and pavements.

My first outing was to the café at Riverside Studios. I was accompanied by two physiotherapists, who brought along a wheelchair so I could rest a couple of times. The rehab activities were great at improving my personal confidence and the staff made it good fun as well.

I was discharged after two months and had nearly two further months of physio and occupational therapy, with daily visits from Mondays to Fridays. The physios and doctors all warned me that I would continue to experience strong fatigue for quite some time, and so it has proved, but it was a small price to pay for recovery.

So, what did I learn? That despite present difficulties, the NHS is wonderful when one is in the system, and that one can transition from good health and fitness to intensive care within days.

I was delighted that I recovered enough to enjoy the celebrations for my ninetieth birthday, in December. I had a party in the House of Lords with family and friends from diverse parts of my life, albeit a few weeks late. Speakers included John O'Farrell, Baroness Angela Smith and John Bercow, and Feargal Sharkey led the guests in a rendition of 'Happy Birthday to You'! I was touched to receive birthday wishes by letter from both previous Labour PMs as well as from John Major.

On 15 June 2025, the BBC broadcast my appearance on *Desert Island Discs*. I had been rather surprised to be invited onto the show, which was recorded a few weeks earlier. I tried to find a piece of music to accompany all the different periods of my life. I settled on Emile Zola's *Germinal* for my book, and chose a pair of walking boots as my luxury item. It was a rewarding experience, and not least because the host Lauren Laverne handled it so well. I was honoured to be on the programme.

V.

Nicholas Winton died on 1 July 2015. I had been to his 106th birthday party a few weeks earlier. He was clearly fading but still intellectually quite sharp. There was a ceremony in Prague to commemorate his life. We had an event at Prague station. I stood on the same platform from which I had departed aged six with my small knapsack, and from which I reached safety, thanks to Nicky and his helpers. The Czech prime minister came along, and we had a short chat. It was a poignant occasion. We then took a train to a village in the countryside, where we planted trees to commemorate Nicky.

He was a great man whose biography has been well written by Barbara, his daughter. Her book provided much of the material on which the film *One Life* is based. Released early in 2024, it tells the story of Nicky's work during the war, with Anthony Hopkins playing the part of the older Nicky. When I first saw the film, I had to rub my eyes to realise that it was not Nicky himself but a brilliant likeness. It was an uncannily accurate portrayal, including Nicky's voice and mannerisms. I found the film intensely moving. Watching it, tears poured down my cheeks. It brought back so many memories. At the second viewing, I thought I'd be hardened to it, but not a bit; tears poured down my cheeks again. My emotional involvement with the film was such that I couldn't judge it by the standards of other films. The film should be shown in schools to educate young people about the Holocaust.

In January 2024, Hella Pick and I were invited by the Bundestag to a series of events in Berlin to commemorate the Kindertransport. Hella was the very distinguished *Guardian* journalist who had come from Austria. There was an exhibition in the German Parliament about several individuals who had reached the UK by Kindertransport from Germany. It was brilliantly documented with copies of letters they had written to their parents or received from them – until they just stopped. We spent two fascinating days and appeared jointly on a panel to answer questions about our journeys to the UK and above all what we thought about the present situation. There had recently been a wave of extreme right-wing demonstrations in various German towns and cities, which had shocked many people. The president of the Bundestag condemned these demos in no uncertain terms. The following day there was a Holocaust Memorial Day event in the Reichstag. Again the president of the Bundestag spoke brilliantly. I was moved, and reminded that Germany had done so much to come to terms with its difficult and tragic past, something that is still not sufficiently widely acknowledged.

Although I had known Hella a little, those two days gave me a chance to get to know her better. She was such an impressive person. I wanted to keep in touch but tragically, before we had a chance to get together, she phoned to cancel because she was unwell and soon after she died.

I believe there is a remarkable contrast between how Germany and Austria have acknowledged their pasts. One only needs to visit the Museum of German History in Berlin and see the models of Auschwitz and hear the stories of what happened to the Jews and others under Nazi rule to give the Germans credit for the way they have come to terms with their history. Initially, the Austrians wanted us to think that they were on the side of the angels all along. But I knew that there had been a stark contrast between Austrian reaction to the Anschluss in 1938 when people cheered Hitler, and the very sombre reaction in Prague to the German invasion in March 1939.

Around the turn of the millennium, and after several visits to the Czech Republic and Austria, I thought I should try to track down my cousins again – the sons of my mother's brother. One was living in Salzburg and the other in Villach. I managed to talk with them by phone and arranged to visit. I knew quite a lot about their lives, but they seemed to know nothing about me. They were taken aback when I showed them a photo of me with the Queen at Hillsborough Castle and told them that I had been in the House of Commons and was now in the Lords. We were sitting in a café in Villach where one of the brothers was a local GP and about to retire. Chatting about my role in politics, the doctor asked why my family left Prague for England in 1939. I was stunned. His question left me completely speechless. How could I start to explain that being Jewish under Nazi occupation was not a recipe for a long life? And did I really need to? While I was pondering how to answer, a patient went up to the doctor, and they started to discuss something. I had lost the moment when I could have addressed his question. They then drove me to the airport. To my lasting regret, I never got back to the issue.

I knew there had been some resentment on my mother's side of the family that she had spent the war years in the UK. There were near-starvation-level food shortages in Austria towards the end of the war, and there seemed to be a perception that we'd had it easy. Her relations possibly also didn't like the fact that she had married a Jew. All this gave me the sense that the Austrians took a long time to come to terms with their pro-Nazi history. Some years ago, I met a man who had been asked to help to de-Nazify Germany in about 1948. I questioned why he had not turned his attention to Austria. His reply was blunt: 'If I had been asked to de-Nazify Austria, there would have been only four and a half Austrians left.' In fairness, the Austrians have more recently begun to come to terms with their past and are making amends for their earlier post-war attitudes.

I have continued to visit the Czech Republic over the years, and witnessed its history unfolding. In 1969, when working for the British Market Research Bureau, I attended a conference in Prague on market research and economic planning. This was a year after the Soviet invasion, and many of the Czechs were expecting to lose their jobs. I spoke to a young publisher, who said he expected to be fired shortly as he was not prepared to publish anything that justified the Soviet invasion. I asked him if it would be better to stay in his job and tone things down a bit, rather than let his job go to a hard-line Communist. His reply was withering: 'That's what they said about collaborating with the Nazis.' I felt very small.

Although I have visited the Czech Republic many times in recent years, it still provokes a profound emotional response. I have on two occasions stayed at the British embassy in Prague, once hosted by the ambassador, the second woman in succession to hold the post. The embassy is a delightful building, just below the castle; there could not be a better place to stay in the whole of Prague. Both times I found myself thinking that it was an amazing place to spend the night for someone who had once been a six-year-old escaping the city.

While I was a minister in Northern Ireland, I was able to meet a hero of mine, President Havel of the Czech Republic. We had a discussion in London in English. He asked me whether I had visited Prague recently, which I had, and what I thought of the city. I replied that there was good and bad, to which he asked me to tell him about the bad. We talked about how Western companies were coming to Prague and redeveloping the beautiful and traditional buildings. The president said that many people were worried about the 'McDonaldisation' of Prague, but when he said so in public speeches, he was accused of bringing socialism into planning. I thought that Havel was a wonderful person and regret that subsequent presidents have not been able to equal his principles and abilities.

On another visit to Prague, to attend the Forum 2000 conference, which was set up to continue the legacy of Havel and is centred around discussions of human rights and democratic values, I was invited to go to Praha-Bubny, a small railway station from which thousands of Jews were taken to the concentration camps. The aim was to establish an interpretation centre there. I said a few words and was critical of the 'refugees are not our problem' attitude of the Czech Republic, Slovakia, Poland and Hungary. They appear to be only interested in welcoming white Christians as refugees. At Praha-Bubny I received a round of applause for saying this, but when I made the same comment at a breakfast at the Foreign Ministry, I sensed there was less enthusiasm for my views. Since then, the politics of the four countries in the Visegrád Group (a cultural and political alliance of the four Central European countries: the Czech Republic, Hungary, Poland and Slovakia) have changed. While Slovakia has moved nearer to the Hungarian position, the Czechs are so far taking a different approach. As regards Poland, their politics seemed to have taken a turn for the better, but recently there has been an electoral reverse.

Around 2016, I finally visited Auschwitz-Birkenau when I was in Kraków for the weekend with my friend Martin, who was a fellow Jewish refugee from Prague. At one point, we stood in front of the pile of suitcases that had belonged to people who had been gassed. I said to Martin, 'I know what you are doing. You are looking to see whether you recognise any of the names on the suitcases.' I was doing it too. I was looking for the initials of my father's cousin and many others. Nobody can fail to be moved, indeed, shattered, by a visit to Auschwitz.

I also visited Theresienstadt (Terezin), the concentration camp in the Czech Republic. Although this was not an extermination camp, many died there, and for others it was a staging post to Auschwitz. I still recall what a gloomy autumn day it was and how utterly depressed I was by the thought of how many people had lost their lives there. When I consider our Jewish friends and relatives in Prague in 1939, they all either managed to flee the country or without exception were sent to camps. Some survived, others were never heard of again. It is something I wish I had told my mother's cousin, the doctor in Austria.

I was delighted to have had my Czech citizenship restored in 2021, as I feel European as well as British. I am glad that I have both a European and a British passport, which allows me to go freely into the European Union following Brexit. My dual citizenship also makes me the first Czech-British member of the House of Lords.

I was born in Czechoslovakia but am grateful to have made Britain my home. I shall always want to say thank you to this country for being terrific to me, and for the opportunities it has offered. Lifelines were provided for me, and in turn, I have tried to provide them for others. My wish and hope for refugees arriving today is that they will have the same welcome and opportunities I received.

My life could have been so different. But I am what circumstances have made me.

Hopes for the Future

As I write this, there are many issues that represent my unfinished political business.

Britain, perhaps more than most nations, was built on migration. This is something that sadly we seem to have forgotten. I look forward to the day when our politicians lead this country towards a more compassionate and human rights-based approach to asylum seekers and refugees, including the implementation of legislation that would enable children to be reunited with their families in the UK. In addition, we need safe and legal routes for asylum seekers to help break the gangs' business model of preying on human despair. We need a more positive policy to help asylum seekers integrate into our country. That means they shouldn't have to wait longer than six months before they have the right to work, enabling them to contribute to society and pay taxes. It also means assisting them in learning English and assisting child refugees to catch up on lost education.

I hope before too long that we will have a government that no longer uses language like 'illegal migrants', 'invaders', or 'country of strangers', because these have an adverse effect on public opinion. I would like development aid to go back to 0.7% of GDP.

I don't believe we can move towards proper human-rights based policies on asylum and refugees without doing so through international cooperation especially with other European countries.

There are other human rights violations that I would also wish to see rectified, including the case of Shamima Begum who left East London to join ISIS as a schoolgirl and who has had her British citizenship taken away. She is not alone. There are others like her, including children, who are effectively stateless. They should, if necessary, face British justice here and not be left in indefinite detention in northern Syria. Surprisingly, an unlikely political consensus has broken out between me and Jacob Rees-Mogg who shares my views on the subject of citizenship stripping.

Looking beyond immigration, I would like to see fundamental changes to the Lords. Titles should be dropped as a preliminary to having an elected second chamber.

I think we should be braver in challenging the part that formal religion plays in our institutions, including in our schools. I would like to see all parents in Northern Ireland have the option of sending their children to an integrated school rather than one broadly defined by religion. In Great Britain, I would like schools here to follow Northern Ireland's integrated model.

Our press needs proper independent regulation. All tax returns should be in the public domain. Foreign donations to political parties and campaigns should be stopped.

We must ensure that the BBC remains an effective public service broadcaster with adequate resources to maintain a powerful world service.

I hope the proposed legislation on assisted dying will soon be on the statute book, as I would not wish others to be denied a right that I would want for myself.

There needs to be more widespread international agreement on banning anti-personnel landmines and cluster bombs.

As regards climate change, we must progress rapidly towards achieving net zero by 2050.

Finally, I believe Brexit has been a complete disaster in economic, political and cultural terms and would like to see Britain rejoin the EU where we belong.

Acknowledgements

I would like to thank all the people involved in bringing this book to life. In other words, Ann Reeder, Emma Shercliff, Sarah Braybrooke, Leonie Lock, Liz Marvin, Jodie Lewis and Candida Jones. In addition, my thanks go to my many friends in the Battersea Labour Party as well as those in the Paddington and Hammersmith & Fulham Labour Parties.

Index